Stars, Staterooms & Stowaways

Anecdotes from
a Colourful Career in Cruising

Gary K Glading

Discovery Books

Stars, Staterooms & Stowaways
Anecdotes from a Colourful Career in Cruising

First published in the United Kingdom in 2010 by Discovery Books
29 Hacketts Lane
Woking
Surrey
GU22 8PP
Tel: 01932 400800
www.discoverybooks.co.uk

ISBN 978-1-902624-03-7

Book design by Julie Mayes, julie@jam-design.co.uk
Edited by Catherine Beattie
Printed and bound in Latvia by InPrint
www.inprint.lv

Dedication

I dedicate this book to the loving memory of
Meg Potts and Willie Baillie and to Peter Allan
for their shining example, which has inspired
me and countless others in our animal welfare work.

Gary Glading

Stars, Staterooms & Stowaways

Anecdotes from
a Colourful Career in Cruising

Gary K Glading

Discovery Books

My thanks

I should like to thank everyone, both people and animals alike, who are featured in the anecdotes that follow. Without them, not only would there be no book to read, but the last 26 years of my life would have been much less colourful and entertaining to recall.

Gary Glading

Contents

Page

Contents *(continued)*

Foreword

It took three planes and over 24 hours for me to reach *MV Arcadia* and one of the warmest welcomes I can remember. Gary was Cruise Director on board and could instantly tell that I'd had a rather rough journey, so after showing me to my cabin, he took me for lunch in one of the ship's elegant restaurants overlooking Acapulco Bay. Within minutes, my stress and fatigue disappeared and a firm friendship had started.

Over the next fortnight we met for lunch, dinner and several cups of hot chocolate and never stopped laughing at each other's anecdotes. I soon discovered what a fascinating career in show business Gary had enjoyed before joining P&O Cruises. This made our mutual bond stronger as we now had one more thing in common.

At that time, Gary was collecting reminiscences from his years on cruise ships and because he trusted my judgement, asked me to read them and give him my honest opinion. I readily admit to having been a bit nervous because I didn't want to disillusion my new friend should they not be to my liking, but happily found them to be sometimes touching, often very funny and always highly entertaining.

Gary and I share a deep love and respect for animals. I was thrilled to learn that all of the royalties from this book will go to his sanctuary for abandoned and abused animals, who now share his delightful home in Italy.

I sincerely hope you will enjoy reading this collection of stories as much as I did, especially if you are lucky enough to be on board a ship where my dear friend Gary Glading is Cruise Director.

Marti Webb
International Musical and Recording Star

Introduction

Who, in their right mind, would choose to look after 32 cats, six donkeys, four goats, three geese, two ducks, two rabbits, a score or so of chickens and a wild boar? Only a dedicated animal lover, for sure!

Ever since I can remember, I have loved animals. One of my earliest memories is of falling asleep snugly cuddled up against the warm belly of a neighbour's Doberman. She was an excellent guard dog and growled at anything or anyone that approached her master's house, but somehow an unsteady toddler with a passion for anything born of fur, feathers or fins didn't represent a threat to her and we became fast friends.

Throughout my teens I lovingly looked after every pet my parents allowed me to have, but it wasn't until I teamed up with British dancer Peter Allan and formed *Glading and Allan*, our on board song and dance act, that my passion for all God's creatures was finally given full rein. I have no idea of the exact number of stray cats and dogs we fed, medicated and snuck back on board in the carefree pre-9/11 days of cruising, but it would be no exaggeration to say it must have been several hundred at least. The amount of food that left the kitchens of the various ships we worked on would impress even the greatest catering houses in the world.

When Peter retired from show business in 1996, I worked as Cruise Director for the Costa Cruise Line, transforming our highly successful double act into a one-man show of international songs. I also returned to my roots as a classical pianist, creating a 'passenger-friendly' piano recital that featured a concert version of a song I wrote for Iris Williams in 1980 (more about this in the following pages).

I was thoroughly enjoying my new-found identity when my boss in the Genoa office suddenly decided to resign and in 1998 I became Costa Cruise Line's new Director of Entertainment. This meant leaving my beloved home in Normandy and moving down to northern Italy.

Because I expected to continue in that role until my retirement, my passion for animal welfare once again took over. In no time at all, the ten cats, one goat and tiny flock of various barnyard fowl from my home in France, became the menagerie described in the first paragraph.

But after eight long years at Costa's head offices in Genoa, I was no longer enjoying my job and left. Then P&O Cruises contacted me and I found myself happily back at sea doing one of the things I like best - entertaining people. I thought I had found my ideal job with this legendary British cruise line, but when the sterling/euro exchange rate dropped dramatically, for the sake of the animals I look after, I had to consider other offers. I accepted Norwegian Cruise Line's proposal and have been contentedly working on their European-based vessels since May 2010.

So who looks after the animal sanctuary whilst I gallivant around the globe on luxurious cruise ships, trying to earn enough to keep everyone in clean straw, properly fed and vaccinated? That's a very good question. A wonderful group of loving friends and family help out whenever possible, but Peter is the shining star undertaking most of the onerous tasks. Since leaving the stage, he has become one of Genoa's most sought-after English teachers and is now a highly respected and popular professor at the city's principal Merchant Naval Academy.

You may ask why any profits from the sale of this book are funding an animal shelter that is already running smoothly? Rising food prices and higher veterinary bills instantly spring to mind, but the main reason is to allow us to welcome more animals to the refuge, animals suffering cruelty, hunger and abuse.

Thank you for buying this book - I hope you enjoy reading my collection of stories from my 26 years in the cruising industry. Your purchase will enable us to help many precious creatures that cannot help themselves. On their behalf, thank you for your support.

Gary Glading

1. The Story Begins.....

When I embarked as an entertainer on my first cruise ship in 1985, I never imagined that more than 20 years later I would still be heavily involved in the cruise industry. Given the tremendous growth in worldwide tourism in the past two decades, cruising has seen unprecedented development at an often-alarming rate. Not only have the ships changed dramatically in that relatively short period of time, but the passengers are no longer just the aged millionaires who populated the great liners of the past. Cruise ships now resemble floating hotels with very little to remind people that they are at sea. Glass lifts and eight-deck atria have replaced the warm wooden panelling and highly polished brass of bygone days. In order to survive and indeed thrive in today's highly competitive market, the profit-driven managers running the business these days have had to cut prices and reluctantly some of the niceties that were once synomonous with cruising in the past. The democratic wave that hit the airline industry in the early 1980s has now engulfed cruising. Many welcome this change, happily turning up at the Captain's Gala Cocktail Party in blue jeans and a tee shirt, while others lament the passing of a more glamorous age, when sequins and black ties were worn at even the most casual affairs.

Since the first transatlantic liners began their regular crossings, celebrities have been associated with cruising. Stars and shipping companies have both benefited from this arrangement. As Cruise Director, I have had the pleasure of interviewing many of the greats from Hollywood's Golden Era, have danced cheek to cheek with others and even helped one or two back to their staterooms after they've had a bit too much to drink. In the pages that follow,

I'll blow away some of the stardust that surrounds some of those famous names and faces.

Security is another area where the world of cruising has changed beyond all recognition. In the halcyon days before 9/11, it was not uncommon for passengers to have friends and family visit them on the ship at our various ports of call. Now all of that is just a fond memory of gentler times. I also remember when wealthy dowagers were never seen on board without their little lap dogs clutched possessively to their ample bosoms. In those innocent days of low-level security and less emphasis on germs and contamination, my own animal involvement was of a more humanitarian nature. There was a constant stream of meat and fish leftovers going from the ships' galleys to my cabin, to be carefully de-boned and put into bags for distribution to the starving cats and dogs awaiting our arrival at the next port. God only knows how long they had waited because their emaciated bodies always looked as if they had never had a full belly in their lives.

By the end of the communist rule in the USSR, blankets, clothes and food were also collected on board and discreetly handed out. Such overt misery always causes a pang in the heart and a lump in the throat. Medicines and basic products like soap or cooking oil were also smuggled ashore. The only in-bound traffic was the occasional cat in such dire need of attention that it could not be abandoned. Some were missing an eye, others had only three paws. All would be clandestinely spirited ashore at the next 'civilised' port and taken directly to a veterinary clinic. After getting all the necessary injections, medication and health certificates, the four-legged stowaway would be hidden in a jacket or bag and set free in my cabin, where my overly-tipped steward remained loyally silent about my furry guest. Those of you who know the copious rewards of saving a stray animal's life, will be heartened by some of the tales in this book featuring these 'adopted orphans'.

Another cruise 'innovation' is that the high-powered marketing experts have collectively decided that passengers should no longer be called passengers - they are now to be called 'guests.' I always thought that guests were people who were invited somewhere for free; at least that is still the case in my home. This attempt at manipulating the patrons' collective mindset hit a record high (or perhaps I should say record low) when I overheard the president of an American cruise line saying to the passengers walking on board one of his ships, 'Welcome home!' I don't know what it's like at your house, but where I live, I don't receive a bill every week for my food and lodging, nor do several thousand other people live there with me.

These days there are cruise options for just about every budget and taste: from one-day cruises to 'nowhere' (so the ship legitimately becomes a floating gambling palace), to around the world cruises lasting over 100 days and all the mainstream one-week or fortnight possibilities in between. Whether going for a cheap and cheerful holiday at sea or opting for the luxury of a penthouse suite on a five-star plus vessel, passengers share one thing in common: they are all people. While that may sound simplistic, the majority of cruise goers resemble each other when it comes down to such basics as food, drink and creature comforts. We all laugh at certain things, we all cry at others and we can all be unreasonable when it comes to eating, drinking or pampering ourselves. This is why this compilation of cruising anecdotes collected over the past 20-plus years will strike a chord in the hearts of all travellers, be they cruisers or landlubbers. On the high seas of the world, in the arid deserts of this planet or the bustling cities of our nations, people interact with people and we are a most fascinating species to study. With that thought in mind, I wish you a most enjoyable look at your fellow man as you discover the world of cruising from an 'insider's' point of view.

2. Taking the Viking by the Horns

As the cruise industry has grown over the years, so has the demand to find new and exciting destinations for well-travelled passengers to discover. Ocean Cruise Lines was known for its inventive itineraries and had a delightful fleet of vessels small enough to visit some of the more out-of-the-way ports, inaccessible to larger cruise ships.

Venezuela's Orinoco River was one such place. After our ship left the bright azure waters of the Caribbean, it was a long, slow sail up the muddy waters of this South American river, which slithers its way through the lush jungle like a giant snake. Once the coastal towns and cities had been left behind, a series of small villages could be noticed, tucked away in the dense foliage lining the parallel riverbanks.

Before long, a miniature flotilla of dugout canoes would suddenly appear one by one from the undergrowth and start their frenetic pursuit of our ship. Because we made a weekly run up the river, these local Indians were as used to seeing us as were we to viewing them. Early in the season, the river pilot told us not to throw food or drink to these tribesmen. If we really wanted to help them, he suggested we should throw bundles of clothing tightly wrapped in heavy plastic bags overboard. Although the natives wore nothing more than a tiny loincloth and a few decorative pieces of jewellery and feathers, they could trade these clothes at the local markets.

This regular collection of clothing parcels soon became a popular event with both crew and passengers, who threw their donations over the side of the ship with one hand and photographed their generosity with the other. The Indians didn't seem to mind as long as this floating 'manna from cruising heaven' kept coming.

In the 1980s, many cruise ships organised a masquerade evening. Passengers created their own costumes making use of copious quantities of crepe paper put at their disposal. Or they slipped on something more elaborate and costly brought from home. Countless rolls of crepe paper were needed each season, but given their compact size, vast quantities could be stocked on board with relatively few problems. Some companies even provided boxes of accessories, such as pirate bandanas and eye patches, Hawaiian leis and plastic bowler hats. These shiny black hats were packaged one inside the other in cartons of 500 and took up little room.

During the previous summer season, the *Ocean Islander* had cruised the Baltic Sea and the Norwegian fjords and an order had been placed for thick paper Viking hats for the big 'Frozen North' deck party. Someone in the main office had over-estimated the number of hats required because there were still scores of boxes of them, which we were asked to recycle during our masquerade evening. We had been asked how many we wanted and thought 250 a feasible number to work through. Such a small batch would be relatively easy to store in our already limited space in the stockroom, especially if all 250 hats fitted into one tidy cardboard box.

Arriving at Barbados on our 'turnaround day,' we could hardly believe our eyes. Stacked a mile high were 20 enormous boxes waiting to be brought aboard. Each box was clearly marked in big bold letters: 'Quality Costume Viking Hats.'

'There must be some mistake,' I told the port agent. 'We ordered 250 party hats, not 2,500.'

'It seemed an awful lot of boxes to me as well,' he replied, 'but when I saw that each box contained only 12 hats, I re-read your order for 250 and realised that you still have another ten hats coming to you.'

'Heaven forbid!' I exclaimed. 'Please give them to your children to use for Mardi Gras.'

The riddle of the boxes was solved when the first one was opened. Inside were two layers of six hats, each hat enveloped in tissue paper and carefully packed. These were cheap paper hats, not the crown jewels, so why all the fuss?

No matter how hard we tried, we could only squeeze four boxes into the stockroom, so the others were temporarily distributed among the staff to be kept in their cabins. These berths were already small and cramped so it wasn't long before the troops began to grumble. I called a meeting to see what could be done and no one came up with a realistic solution, until a disgruntled voice in the back said 'Why don't we just throw them overboard?'

'That's it!' I cried. 'That's exactly what we'll do.'

'I was only kidding,' continued the dozy voice. 'It's illegal to dump things like this at sea.'

'I know,' I said, half giggling to myself. 'I don't intend to dump them at sea.'

'Well, no port is going to allow you to dump them on the quayside without paying a fine,' the devil's advocate continued.

'I know that as well,' I admitted.

'So where on earth *are* you going to dump them?' queried the rest of the group in one loud chorus.

'Up the Orinoco,' I answered with a big grin on my face. 'Can't you just see our little native friends' faces when they open up these boxes? They'll make great bargaining material for them at the local market next week.'

Our next trip up the Orinoco proceeded like the earlier ones with passengers and crew launching clothes parcels overboard and taking photographs as the natives manoeuvred their canoes and snatched each and every bag afloat. No one thought any more about the hats or our little Indian friends throughout the rest of the cruise.

The following week, I was busy in the office, so wasn't out on deck for the usual clothes launching party. One of my staff called me to come outside right away.

'I'm very busy. Is it urgent?' I asked, rather impatiently.

'It's not urgent,' replied my colleague, 'but if you miss this show, you'll never forgive yourself.'

Curious and armed with my camera, I ran up onto the deck. I had never seen it so full, nor heard so much chatter before. I made my way through the crowds to the guardrail and could not believe what I saw. The entire river behind the ship was covered in the largest number of canoes I had ever seen. Each canoe was packed with naked brown-bodied Indians sporting nothing more than a smile and a paper Viking hat! It was one of the most surreal scenes I have ever witnessed. This ludicrous picture was funny enough, but the proverbial icing on the cake was the words of one of our American passengers.

Turning to her husband she said, 'I wonder how *The National Geographic* will explain this when they get my photos!'

3. Good Things Come in Small Packages

For the first 11 years of my cruising career, I was part of a song and dance double act known as *Glading and Allan*. Peter Allan was a consummate dancer with a good singing voice who had worked with me at the Paris Lido, while I am a singer/pianist with basic dance skills. When the Lido created a touring troupe to publicise their Paris and Las Vegas shows around the world, the producers created specific numbers for us to perform to show off our well-matched talents. After four years of travelling the globe as the headliners of that revue show, we accepted an offer to perform a two-man show on a French cruise ship. That first contract was to become the start of a whole new career for both of us and the beginning of our international animal welfare work at sea.

Within a few years, I had become a Cruise Director, but also continued to work as part of the *Glading and Allan* duo. This extra work meant that I could no longer wander ashore as often as before, so my involvement in the stray animal feeding was often reduced to de-boning meat and fish leftovers and tearing them into bite-size pieces. Whenever time permitted, I accompanied Peter on his humanitarian work of feeding the hungry cats and dogs that populated most of the big ports. On the day we visited Yalta in the Ukraine, my workload kept me imprisoned in my small, cluttered office.

On that cruise we had a guest entertainer called Nyta Doval who was a Czechoslovakian countess who spoke and sang flawlessly in eight languages. She was also an animal lover and had already rescued a large number of weak and sick strays. This particular afternoon, she and Peter made their way down the gangway carrying heavily laden plastic bags in each hand. Nyta had already bribed the Soviet customs officials earlier that day, so they glumly waved her and Peter through their checkpoint.

Two hours later I returned to my cabin to get some paperwork and found a note on the bed saying, 'Whatever you do, don't go into the bathroom!' It was signed by Peter. Now, if you had been in my place, what would you have done? Exactly! I opened the bathroom door before you could count to three. There I saw the most precious little ginger kitten looking up at me with one eye open, the other caked over with infection. My heart melted. I gently scooped him up and he started to purr loudly as he rubbed his tiny face against the palm of my hand. Just then I heard the cabin door open and close with a bang.

'Oh, my God, Nyta! He's found the kitten,' Peter blurted out breathlessly. 'I can explain everything,' he ventured as he entered the bathroom.

'There's no need to,' I replied. 'Little Yalta here has already told me all there is to know.'

The next half hour was spent washing him in warm, soapy water and trying to pick all the fleas out of his matted fur. Once that was done, we bathed his bad eye in camomile. The hard crust that had formed fell away, but we soon realised that the eyeball itself was no longer in the socket. The infection must have burst his eye, leaving just an open wound. At the next port where we were sure to find a vet, we smuggled Yalta ashore for his injections, medicine and health certificates, and then snuck him back on board the same way. With his major health problems taken care of, he started to fill out a bit, thanks to a softhearted chef in the main galley with a phenomenal memory. Each evening in the restaurant, our waiter would take the order, and then ask what 'Signor Gatto' (Mr Cat) would like. Being a vegetarian myself, I ordered whatever food I thought a cat might enjoy. More often than not, a completely different dish was brought out in a little Tupperware container with a note from the chef saying, 'Signor Gatto had lamb last night, so I've given him turkey tonight' or 'Today's fish isn't fresh, it's frozen, so I've wrapped up some delicious chicken for him.'

As Yalta grew bigger and stronger, he also grew more playful. His favourite game was playing 'the angry cat.' He never scratched or hissed, even in jest, but just hunched up his back like the cats on Halloween cards and walked slowly sideways towards his 'victim.' His tail would be straight as a rod and his head lowered with his single eye fixed in a mock-angry stare. If one didn't know what a sweet-natured feline he was, this might have been quite frightening.

Yalta settled incredibly well into his new life at sea and had many 'aunts and uncles' who regularly came to play with him during their work breaks. Soon only a few days remained before the end of our contract, so we requisitioned a large cardboard box to carry Yalta home in when the time came. Air holes were made and small plastic dishes found for his food and water during the trip. One evening after our gala evening performance, we were about to go to bed when the emergency alarm went off. We both froze, waiting anxiously for the announcement to tell us exactly what kind of danger we were in.

'Fire! Fire! All crew to their emergency stations immediately!' came the voice over the ship's loudspeakers.

I grabbed my bathrobe and lifejacket and headed for the door since I would be needed on the bridge. Peter's emergency duties were to help the passengers into their life vests and keep everyone calm, so he also grabbed his lifejacket, and then stopped.

'What about Yalta? He asked with a frightened look in his eyes.

'Just put him in his box and take him with you. Leave everything else here and get up to the lifeboats as quickly as you can,' I replied, as I exited the cabin.

When I reached the bridge the captain told me that the back decks were on fire and that due to the heavy smoke, our fire squad had not yet managed to extinguish the blaze. To make matters worse, several canisters of gas had been taken on board the previous day for some welding work that needed to be done. These gas bottles were on the deck where the fire was raging. The captain very bluntly told me that unless the fire could be brought under control in the next few minutes, the ship would explode.

I made the required tannoy announcements, calmly asking the passengers to assemble at their lifeboat stations, donning their life vests. Once I had done all I could, I went out onto the wing of the bridge to check that my orders had been carried out quickly, efficiently and serenely one deck below.

It was a beautiful, warm, starry night, so this unexpected tragedy seemed quite out of place. Everyone had reacted magnificently: no shouting, no pushing, and no panic whatsoever. From my vantage point I spotted Peter as he helped the guests on with their lifejackets. As hard as I strained my eyes, I couldn't see Yalta's cardboard box anywhere. I knew Peter would never have left him in the cabin, but couldn't imagine where he was. All of a sudden my attention was drawn to an elderly lady turning around rather brusquely with an indignant look on her face. She said something sharply to a younger woman, then, oddly, they both burst out laughing. The younger woman raised her nightgown slightly to reveal the cardboard box straddled between her feet. I later found out that Yalta had been attracted by all the movement outside his box and stretched his little paw through one of the air holes, grabbing the passing pyjamas and nightdresses, much to the surprise of those wearing them.

Since I lived to tell this tale, you will have deduced that the fire was eventually put out and we returned home safely at the end of our contract as planned. Yalta was greeted with the usual sniffing of the hindquarters by his curious, but friendly feline brothers and sisters and was fully accepted as a member of the family within days. He soon grew into a robust, but tenderhearted ginger tom. Before he was healthy enough to be neutered, he mated with a wild cat living in the woodshed behind our house. One day he came into the kitchen with a very weak little kitten in his mouth. We gave her some food and put her in a basket near the radiator to keep warm. Yalta seemed pleased with this arrangement, but his insistent meowing and scratching at the front door indicated he wanted to go out. Once outside, he kept crying and turning around to look at us. He evidently wanted us to follow him. He led us through the garden to the woodpile where we found his mate and her other kittens all dead. We gathered them up and took them all and the surviving kitten to the vet right away. He confirmed that the mother cat had inadvertently killed herself and her litter minus one, by bringing home a poisoned mouse for them to eat. The vet treated Yalta's daughter successfully and from that day on, they were inseparable.

Yalta's paternal/maternal instincts went as far as raising a pair of orphaned ducklings. It was comical watching him groom them like kittens or when they happily fell asleep against his soft, furry belly when tired. This unlikely trio drifted apart only when the ducklings were old enough to start preening themselves. After all Yalta's loving attention, they repaid the favour by attempting to groom him 'duck-style,' pulling at his fur as they pulled at their loose feathers. This was not a pleasant experience for a longhaired cat, so

Yalta soon gave his adopted offspring the extra space any wise parent gives a badly behaved pubescent teenager.

As the years went by and some of the older cats passed away, Yalta proudly became the highly respected and dearly loved elder of the pack. His incredible adventure lasted for 16 years and took him from the poverty of a Black Sea port in the former Soviet Union, to a luxurious cruise ship, then to a French manor and finally to a villa in the mountains of northern Italy. Throughout his life he was greatly loved by all his two and four-legged family and is still sorely missed by us all.

4. Lucky for Some, Unlucky for Others

ailors are without a doubt among the world's most superstitious people. Certain beliefs and observances are universal whereas others depend on the nationality of the seaman. The Greeks and the Italians are top of the list when it comes to being superstitious. Their philosophies are a combination of Christian doctrine and pagan ritual. The sign of the cross is often followed by some knuckle-rattling knocking on wood. One of the oddest superstitions on many ships of different nationalities is the passing of the saltshaker from one person to another at the dining table. It must not be handed over directly, but released by the giver and placed on the table within reach of the other person. Dire consequences will inevitably occur should anyone on board a ship be foolish enough to tempt fate and go against this fundamental 'law of the sea.'

At first, this seems silly and almost a heresy, but anyone working on ships for more than a few weeks, finds himself following these ridiculous habits. One of my favourite captains was from Sorrento. As I said, most Italian sailors are superstitious, but the further south you travel in that beguiling land, the more intense and bizarre the superstitions become, as this captain proved on many occasions.

The luxurious *Silver Wind* was built in Genoa and launched in January 1995 by Silversea Cruises. A large group of us were on board for the last two months of her construction to follow the progress of her fitting out. In most naval yards, things go 'missing' during the building of any type of ship, from submarines to cruise ships, but I have never seen anything like the stealing that went on in Genoa. Televisions, refrigerators, cutlery and furniture were all on the list of items delivered, but not found on board. One trick that we soon cottoned onto, was presenting a room for verification. Some public rooms had thousands of tiny light bulbs on the ceiling, walls and around the edges of the floor. During the final inspection when all the specifications were checked and signed for, the bulbs would be fully lit with magical effect. The next day, however, there wouldn't be a single bulb in that room; they had all been unscrewed for use in another lounge being readied for inspection. Even when this ruse was discovered and excuses found for this 'unintentional oversight,' something else would crop up and the game started all over again.

January 14th was the date we had to respect no matter what happened. That was the day chosen by the owners for the christening of the ship in Civitavecchia, Italy. The local cardinal was booked to officiate, the grandstands had been ordered and all the usual VIPs and press alerted. Any change of plan would create total chaos, and in Italy, total chaos is something that makes even battle-hardened generals cry like babies.

The work at the shipyard was advancing nicely, but at the last minute a few disagreements between the builders and the future owners threatened to delay the entire project. Most people are unaware that when a ship is constructed, it belongs to the shipyard until the prospective owners agree that everything has been carried out according to the specifications of the signed contract. In the case of a vessel with Italian registry, the actual transfer of ownership takes place in the city where the ship is to be registered. With the *Silver Wind*, that city was Palermo, Sicily. So once the major contentions were worked out, both parties flew down to Palermo for the official signing of the deeds.

The signing procedures were planned for 12th January. This allowed plenty of time for the *Silver Wind* to travel down to Civitavecchia for her christening, scheduled for the morning of the

14th. What everyone involved had totally ignored or forgotten, was that the date the new ship was to make her first journey outside her 'birth place' was Friday the 13th. Such a date sends chills down many a landlubber's spine, but to an Italian sea captain from Sorrento, this fluke of the calendar was an evil omen from the very depths of Hades. Once this unlucky date was brought to everyone's attention, it was decided to have the paperwork in Palermo done late morning. The papers could be flown back to Genoa early afternoon so the ship could be on her way before sunset on the 12th. This solution placated many frayed nerves and would have been marvellous *if* implemented. Unfortunately, last minute business delayed the signing, delaying the return to Genoa and making our Sorrentine captain frantic with impending doom. 6.00pm became 7, 7.00pm turned into 8, and by 8.30pm, the captain was threatening to crash the ship against the harbour wall so the inevitable sinking of this 'newborn' would result in the smallest loss of life possible.

When the breathless runners arrived at the bottom of the halfway hoisted gangway and jumped on board, the captain with his ever-ready binoculars saw what the men had in their hands. He gave the order to bring the gangway all the way in and to rev-up the engines. Within minutes and comfortably before our midnight deadline, *Silver Wind* was finally underway. Only God and our captain know exactly what our speed was as we left the docks, but Genoese sailors are still talking about the highest wake Genoa harbour has ever seen.

5. Allons, Enfants de la Patrie!

We have all lived through dramatic situations where imminent danger or looming tragedy means the total absence of laughter or even a coy smile. Assuming we survive the actual disaster, it can take anything from five minutes to a few years before we can look back on the situation with any good humour. One such incident took place during a world cruise undertaken by the French cruise ship *Mermoz*.

The ship had dropped anchor off the coast of Bali, forcing those who wished to go ashore to use the new tender boats that were part of *Mermoz's* recent refit. The pride on the officers' faces was on display for all to see, as gleaming in the morning sunshine, the boats were gently lowered to the smooth surface of the tropical waters below for the first time. The tendering operations proceeded like clockwork all day long, so no one could be blamed for not anticipating what was about to happen.

As I had never visited this port before, I decided to go ashore after completing my paperwork. The passengers remaining on board were enjoying whatever activity they had chosen to follow.

As the sun began to set in the beautiful western sky, the wind started to build. At first, it was just a light breeze, making me wish I had taken my jacket. By the time I was ready to return to the ship and was awaiting the next tender on the port's wooden pier, the sea was noticeably rougher with the mounting strength of the wind. The sailors on board the tender made several attempts to throw the tie-up ropes ashore, but the cords kept falling short of the outstretched hands waiting to catch them because of the wind. Finally the tender managed to dock and we loaded the prescribed number of passengers. We were casting off, when the back of the boat suddenly dropped in the water by at least two feet. Everyone turned around to see that four or five people had jumped on board as we pushed away from the pier. The officer in charge gave them a stern look and was about to turn the boat around and force them to disembark. But when he saw how many people were still impatiently waiting on the pier ready to jump on board like the others, he decided against going back and headed for the *Mermoz*.

With its flat bottom and squared-off bow set on a sharp angle, the tender boat looked like the baby cousin of the World War II landing crafts that the Allies used in the D-day landings in Normandy. Everything was fine until we went around the point of the headland and left the protection it had offered us so far. Although the waves were hardly tsunami size, they were just that little bit too high for the weight we were carrying. With the arrival of each new wave, a few buckets' worth of water entered the craft from the bow. The helmsman immediately asked the passengers to move toward the back of the boat so that the bow would be higher out of the water, but that only made the water come in from the back as well. By this time, we were all ankle deep in warm seawater and still much too far from the *Mermoz* for comfort. The officer desperately tried to radio the ship, but there was no answer. The flare we shot up only succeeded in bringing faintly heard cheers from the native people on the distant shore.

It was at that point that I asked the passengers for help bailing the water out. If we could at least keep the water level inside the boat from increasing, we might manage to limp back to the ship. For reasons unknown, my suggestion was treated as something tantamount to high treason. Instead of scooping up the invading waters and dumping them over the side, my fellow travellers collectively chose to completely ignore me. One by one, they stood up and began to sing *La Marseillaise!* I didn't know whether to laugh, cry or join in, but common sense told me just to keep on bailing.

It must have been a full 15 minutes before I saw the powerful tender of a rival cruise line speeding towards the pier we had just left, what seemed a lifetime ago. As no help was forthcoming from our own vessel, I took it upon myself to shout and wave my arms at the other tender. At first, there was no reaction; it plowed on through the rough seas toward the dock. Then suddenly she veered around with such gusto that I half expected to see her passengers unceremoniously dumped into the churning waters. Within minutes, our saviours were busily tying-up our pathetic, waterlogged tender behind their super-charged engines and our humiliating tow back to our ship was underway. The lusty voices that had fervently belted out the stirring words of their national anthem only a few minutes before, had now fallen silent and remained that way until they reached the safety of *Mermoz's* gangway. At that point they rekindled their zeal. Shouted threats of a mutiny against the captain and calls for a collective lawsuit could be heard echoing through the now dark Indonesian heavens.

There was never any official recognition of what had happened that night, or of the inadequate design of our tender boats. When we reached our next major port of call, I noticed that the boats were quietly replaced with the traditional model. I don't think the officers in charge appreciated the crew's warped sense of humour as they hummed Elvis Presley's old hit *Love me Tender* each time they climbed aboard.

6. Hamburg by Night

During one of the summer seasons that the *Ocean Princess* cruised the Baltic Sea ports, we made a single stop in Hamburg. It was not a city we visited on our regular runs as docking is rather expensive and it is so far up the Elbe River that sailing time is lost leaving and rejoining the Baltic. The city is often done as part of a trans-Kiel Canal cruise. As it was our inaugural call at Hamburg, the organisation of the land operations was not as efficient as usual with only general information available on excursions. The daytime tours were self-explanatory, but the *Hamburg by Night* one was less evident.

We were supposed to tour the city by coach enjoying the highlights of the illuminated city centre, before heading up to the Reeperbahn or 'red light district' of town. We would walk along this infamous street to a beer garden where we could take in the bawdy music of a local 'oompah' band as we downed our German lager and munched on our salty pretzels. After that we were to attend a typical 'risqué' show at one of the many small clubs lining the side streets off the main thoroughfare.

Our shore excursion manageress was quite frank with our passengers when describing these tours. When she mentioned the 'risqué' show at the end of the evening tour, there was a lot of sniggering and muffled laughter, but no one questioned exactly what was meant by the vague term 'risqué'. As most of our guests on that trip were definitely in the grey-haired brigade, we did not expect a big turnout. To our surprise, it was a complete sell-out. The Hamburg port agent suggested that, although it was not a terribly dangerous part of the city, as there were always pick-pockets, drunks and other unsavoury characters to watch out for, it would be advisable to have as many of the male staff as possible accompany the tour.

The beginning of our nocturnal excursion was pure bliss. The fine stonework of the Neo-Gothic buildings we drove past stood out in the soft-focus spotlights almost coming alive against the darkened summer skies. We even enjoyed our enthusiastic beer hall entertainment. I was starting to relax as we safely reached our final destination of the evening - the venue of the 'risqué' show. You could feel the excitement building up as our septuagenarians speculated among themselves about how much the performers would reveal. Then the lights dimmed and some tacky recorded music was blasted through the ancient sound system and the audience settled down in breathless anticipation.

For the next hour and a half we were treated to some of the sleaziest, most disinterested live sex imaginable. The room was so small that anyone in the back row could easily count the holes in one of the stripper's tights. As these ended up being her entire costume, it made the entire affair even more disreputable. I was sitting on the left side of the amphitheatre-like club, so could scrutinise the faces of the passengers sitting opposite me. Throughout the show, I saw looks of horror, glazed stares of disbelief and just a few eyes registering delight. I thought about our ride back to the ship. There would either be a total embarrassed or indignant silence, or everyone would be chattering like monkeys about the night's events. As it turned out, a stone-cold silence made the temperature of the bus drop to below zero. The 15-minute drive to the harbour felt like three hours. Just before arriving at the ship, a lady at the back said in a loud whisper to her half-asleep husband, 'I thought there'd be more singing and dancing in the show.'

With that, the whole bus broke-out in peals of laughter. Thanks to that lady, a totally disastrous evening was avoided.

7. Who said 'Size Doesn't Matter'?

Some years ago, I was the Cruise Director of the *Silver Wind* as she made an autumn sailing from Europe to America. To entice passengers to make the crossing with us, the company came up with the idea of inviting a number of well-known film and theatrical stars as VIP guests. Among them was the movie star Brenda Vaccaro whose role in the 1960's classic *Midnight Cowboy* brought her international fame. Silversea's management decided to dedicate one day of the cruise to each celebrity. I interviewed them in the morning and then in the afternoon they read excerpts from the diaries of late 19th and 20th century immigrants who shared a common heritage. Brenda's reading of the Italian steerage class passengers' experiences was particularly poignant and her interview absolutely brilliant. She later told me she had never felt so comfortable when being questioned before a live audience. To thank me for putting her at her ease, she invited me to dine with her and Guy, her French husband.

Brenda is such a fun and expansive person that it is impossible not to have fun with her. She has a rich, husky tone when she speaks, which is perfect for her many television ads and voiceovers, but it is only when she laughs that you fully appreciate her unique voice. Throughout the crossing I had many opportunities of sharing a meal, coffee or a drink with Brenda and we quickly became friends. She told me all about her long live-in relationship with Michael Douglas, at a time when she was a bigger star than he and when 'shacking up' together was still frowned upon. According to Brenda, Michael's parents never really sanctioned their love affair. Was this because of the young couple's religious differences, their disparity in celebrity status, or just that Kirk and his wife held fast to their old-fashioned values? We'll never know, but it was fun hearing about Brenda and Michael's wild parties and escapades at a time when I was still in grade school.

Brenda's husband Guy was much younger than her and prided himself on keeping fit. Since he spent a lot of time in the ship's gym, Brenda tried to keep up with him (or perhaps she wanted to keep an eye on him). She even went on a very strict diet to make herself more appealing to the youthful Romeo she had recently married. She was in serious training for her upcoming film appearance as Barbra Streisand's best friend in *The Mirror has Two Faces*. That movie was a sort of *Ugly Duckling* remake with Barbra as the mousey introvert whose incredible transformation seduces and ultimately wins over Jeff Bridges. Anyone with an interest in modern films will be aware that the immensely talented Barbra Streisand is reported to be a demanding and domineering figure on the set, especially when she also directs and produces, as was the case in *The Mirror has Two Faces*. Brenda told me she regularly received phone calls from Barbra with specific instructions about how to read certain lines of the script, how to wear her hair, which make-up was acceptable and so on.

One evening when dining with Brenda and Guy, the maitre d' came over to tell Brenda that she had an urgent call from Hollywood. As we were in the middle of the Atlantic at the time, placing such a call and then holding the line while Brenda was paged and taken to the ship's radio room would have cost the caller a small fortune.

There was no problem about Brenda's dinner going cold because she had ordered a large, but very simple salad plate. Guy and I had been feeling guilty about eating so much food in front of Brenda at previous meals, that this evening we had also ordered a big salad to keep her company as she struggled to reduce her weight. As soon as Brenda left the table, Guy leant forward and said, 'that will be Barbra again. Brenda won't be back for at least ten or 15 minutes, so if we play our cards right, we can eat some real food while she's on the phone and go back to our salads when she returns.'

'Great idea!' I said, motioning to the waiter to come over to the table. We both filled up our glasses with some delicious red wine and silently toasted our conniving complicity. Five minutes later our waiter returned with two plates piled high with appetising fare. Just as he placed the food before us, I saw Brenda come charging into the restaurant like an enraged bull.

'Who was that on the phone, darling?' asked Guy in a timid half-whisper.

'It was that *#*+%* Barbra again! Do you know what she had the balls to say?' Brenda replied, without giving us time to answer. 'She said, 'I hope you're eating up on the ship because I need you to be grotesquely fat so that I look young and slender next to you.' Imagine that! How could she know I've been on a diet?' she continued, talking more to herself than to us. 'That #*@%+* must have a second set of eyeballs in her head! Well, if she wants fat, I'll give her fat! Waiter!' she shouted, 'get rid of this frigging rabbit food and bring me a real dinner!' Turning to Guy and me she said with a wry smile, 'An actress has to make so many sacrifices for her art, doesn't she?'

With that we all burst out laughing and clinked our wine glasses together in a heartfelt toast to one amazing lady - Miss Brenda Vaccaro.

8. Bridge Over Troubled Waters

Anyone who has ever been at a bridge table anywhere in the world for more than a few minutes has no doubt witnessed (if not participated in) a 'discussion'. Not an argument, mind you, just a discussion, the type you have with your spouse in company. The temperature of these discussions depends on the presumed expertise of the player doing most of the shouting or sanctimonious lecturing. Real bridge experts tend to get on with it, quietly showing their bravura through their play, unless asked to give constructive criticism for the benefit of novices.

Every summer for four years, Peter and I had a four to six week contract on Cunard's *Vistafjord* as their 'international act'. In addition to the mainstay of British and American passengers, there were many German-speakers and we had to tailor our repertoire to satisfy everyone. Being a guest artiste, I had no other official duties, so the contract was something of a busman's holiday. I could discreetly move about the ship unrecognised until we had performed our first show.

I thoroughly enjoy playing bridge and willingly play with people of all levels. For me, it is an entertaining mental exercise and I never get upset over the outcome, always assuming my partner is doing his or her best. I regularly offered to play in the ship's afternoon tournaments if the bridge teachers on board required a 'fourth' at any of the tables. I was usually placed with a German, as those that showed up often needed a little translation from time to time.

It was on one such afternoon that I heard one of the most comical verbal exchanges. It was between a Texan and an Englishman. In order to fully savour the flavour of their respective accents, imagine the Texan with the voice of President George Bush and the Englishman as comedian Terry Thomas.

In bridge, while the actual playing of the cards is the same, there are several systems for bidding the hand. Without going into too much detail, most Americans play American Standard and most British people play Acol. The fundamental differences are quite evident, but confuse some people.

Two or three times during the tournament, the Texan loudly called the director to the table. No one else in the room could hear what was wrong, as tournaments are as solemn as a Requiem Mass, but it was obvious to all that the Texan was agitated.

Before long, the fireworks began, and we all had front row seats. It quickly became clear that the Texan was accusing the Englishman of cheating and no amount of explanation could persuade him that the British bidding system was legal, if it existed at all. Feeling himself cornered, he finally bellowed out, 'Ah say when ya in Amerka, ya play lak thu 'Amerkins.'

'That's just it,' retorted Her Britannic Majesty's subject, 'we're *not* in America.'

'Well, Coo-nard's an Amerkin cumpny, innit?' he queried with mock innocence, feeling sure he had won the tussle.

'My...good...man,' blurted out the Brit, struggling not to unstiffen his stiff upper lip in public, 'Cunard is a BRRRRRITISH company!'

The rolled 'R's' served as a sort of rapid duel-inviting slap, but it was too late for the defeated southerner to accept the challenge. Once again, Britannia *did* rule the waves.

9. The Road to Zanzibar

The very mention of the some places conjures up vivid images in our minds. Whether these mental pictures come from photographs we have seen, books we have read, or just the outer reaches of our imaginations, names like Timbuktu, Outer Mongolia, Madagascar and Zanzibar have the power to create an instant longing for discovery deep within us.

I have yet to experience the wonders of Outer Mongolia or Timbuktu, but have visited Madagascar and Zanzibar on several occasions. I must confess that I am the type of traveller that, while not blind to poverty, dirt and decrepitude, is interested in just about everything I see. Everything is new whether you have seen it before or not. The weather can be different, or the lighting, or even the company you are with. This does not mean that I keep my eyes open and my heart closed. I am the kind of 'idiot' that feeds the stray dogs and cats, gives something to the poor or infirm and often carries a feeling of helplessness at not being able to do enough to alleviate all the suffering I encounter; yet even these upsetting spectacles add to the richness of the tapestry of travel and make me want to carry on seeing what's behind the next hill, and the next, and the next.

Of course, not all cruise passengers have my view of the world. Some are uncomfortable and discontented if not in air conditioned comfort listening to their native language spoken flawlessly on the latest microphone system. Many are the times when I have nearly bitten a hole right through my lip hearing someone say, 'I don't know why we stopped here, there's nothing to see.'

I remember a comment from one such passenger and each time I return to Zanzibar I smile all over again at its pure innocence. For those of you who don't know Zanzibar, it is dirty and does have its poor, but is tremendously rich in architecture, heritage and the exciting colours and culture of East Africa.

Our city tour was carried out in a small mini-van with room for eight, but with ten of us alarmingly crammed in. There was no air conditioning, no microphone and no end to the complaining of those in my group. The exceedingly high temperature, combined with the stench during our visit to the local open-air market, had almost created a revolution on our little bus. When we eventually made it back to the ship, I was treated to a variety of grumblings, threats and distasteful remarks. One woman unwittingly went right to the root of her fellow-travellers' disappointment with Zanzibar with her timeless comment, 'I really can't imagine why Bob Hope, Bing Crosby, and Dorothy Lamour would ever want to come here in the first place.'

Thanks a lot Hollywood!

10. And Now We Present......

As a dedicated animal lover, I hesitate to relate this next anecdote that took place on a lovely ship called the *Ocean Pearl*. We were sailing to some of the lesser-known and mercifully less tourist-filled islands of Indonesia. The French cruise company Paquet had recently taken over Ocean Cruise Lines and many of the top Paquet 'brass' were on board to observe and implement changes they felt were urgent. As you can imagine, everyone who had been with the old company was anxious to make a favourable impression on the new owners. Among these French VIPs was Monique, the head of entertainment for the new lines. She was an avid animal lover and had done a lot of animal charity work.

On the afternoon before the first show Peter and I were performing for our new bosses, all the staff members who spoke more than just English were recruited to accompany a planned excursion and translate for our foreign guests. The only transport on the island, other than a few rickety old bicycles, was some open flatbed trucks normally used to take pigs and goats to the weekly market. A series of rough wooden planks had been nailed down in the back as a sort of temporary seating. I had to shout in three languages above the deafening noise of an ancient Ford motor to be heard by my dust-covered passengers. Somehow, we all managed to return safely to the ship after our adventure. I had to prepare for our show, so hadn't had time to chat with the other guides to see whether their day had been as eventful as mine.

One of my duties as Assistant Cruise Director was presenting the evening shows, even when I performed in them. On this particular evening, Monique, Paquet's entertainment manager who had worked with us on the *Mermoz* several years earlier, offered to compere the show for me.

After the band played their overture and the ballet performed their high-energy opening number, Monique was about to announce us, when I heard the audience suddenly go quiet. Instead of the usual off-stage microphone presentation we were used to, I saw the stage lights go up and watched Monique slowly walk to the centre of the stage. She began to speak and her voice took on the tone that priests and preachers use at funerals and other solemn occasions. She explained to the audience that she had accompanied the afternoon excursion to the island. She was enjoying the magnificent scenery and glorious sunshine when quite unexpectedly, a small pig ran in front of the truck she was travelling in and was instantly killed. At that point she completely broke down and sobbed loudly into the microphone. The room was a-buzz with gasps of horror as everyone started relating their own experiences to their neighbours.

After what seemed ages, Monique finally composed herself. Then, slowly walking into the shadows of the still grief-struck room, she simply and quietly announced, 'Ladies and Gentlemen, *Glading and Allan!*'

Had we been serving bagels at Yasser Arafat's birthday party, the reception could not have been cooler.

11. Diving in at the Deep End

Few international stars were as iconic as the lovely Esther Williams. Hollywood's Golden Age saw truckloads of highly talented singers, actors, cowboys and comedians, but only one lady who took a simple swimming pool and made an entire career around its heavily chlorinated water.

I had the pleasure of travelling with Esther on one of *Royal Odyssey's* memorable star-studded transatlantic crossings. Despite the extra pounds that now filled out her famous silhouette, she was still a beautiful woman with sparkling eyes and a zest for life that made her seem at least 15 years younger than she actually was.

We all sat enthralled in the ship's comfortable cinema, applauding picture after picture starring this delightful legend. Even after the enthusiastic reaction to her films, nothing prepared us for the disarming and thoroughly charming subject of that afternoon's interview.

Esther's total candour was refreshing and her warmth infectious. She instantly became not only everyone's favourite star, but their best friend as well. My actual interview lasted only about thirty minutes, but the question and answer session that followed was almost twice as long. The passengers just couldn't get enough of this familiar and well-loved personality.

Esther told us about how she had started her career as a model for a department store because women's sports were only on an amateur basis at that time. She admitted she would have loved to have represented the United States in international swimming championships, a dream that would belong to a future generation. She made the audience squeal with laughter when she repeated her future husband Fernando Lamas' marriage proposal to her:

'Let me take you away from all this,' he murmured in his suave South American accent.

'Take me away from all what?' Esther had replied, perplexed. 'If you mean all the luxury, comfort and wealth my career has brought me, then, no thanks!'

Fernando's macho, Latino ego was dented, but not enough for him to give up his pursuit of MGM's stunning and well-established leading lady. Both stars had been married before: Esther to an American football player, Fernando to Arlene Dahl, and each had children from those previous relationships. Esther was close to her stepson Lorenzo Lamas who was making quite a name for himself acting on a popular television show. Unfortunately, her own son, who accompanied her on this nostalgic cruise to New York City, had inherited none of his mother's innate class or charm and was never seen without a beer bottle in his hand. His loud-mouthed interjections during her interview were neither welcome nor of interest to anyone but himself.

The television series *Dallas* was all the rage at the time, so the audience was interested to hear about Howard Keel, one of Esther's former co-stars who played JR's father in the soap. Earlier in the day, we had been treated to a showing of *Pagan Love Song*, the movie Esther and Howard made in 1950. One lady in the audience asked if there were any behind the scenes scoops Esther could let us in on. Esther answered, 'Did anyone notice anything unusual about the swimming stroke Howard and I were doing in the picture?'

The question was greeted with silence, prompting her to continue, 'Well, it was the sidestroke. My co-stars and I usually did the Australian crawl or the breaststroke, so our faces kept out of the water and provided an easy shot for the cameramen. I'm probably telling tales out of school here, but I'm sure Howard won't mind. After all, it certainly hasn't stopped him having one of the greatest and longest careers in Hollywood history. Put very simply, Howard Keel has a withered arm - the type that doesn't fully develop. In order to hide his deformity, we had to do the sidestroke on just one side, so that Howard's weaker arm was always under the waterline. If you think about all his other films and television appearances, he always wears a long-sleeved shirt or some type of jacket or coat.'

This revelation had everyone in the audience skimming through Howard Keel's most famous films in their minds: *Showboat, Annie Get Your Gun, Seven Brides for Seven Brothers* and *Calamity Jane.*

Esther went on to give us the inside story on some of her trickier film shoots. Her own particular physical handicap was severe myopia, or as she put it: 'I'm blind as a bat, so we'd often have to re-shoot something if I swam out of the camera angle or if my dive was not on centre.'

She also explained how her hair always managed to look so good when she rose from the deep like some Neptunium goddess. Several different products and processes had been experimented with, but a solution made from Vaseline and other ingredients gave the requisite look time after time. The spectacular scenes where lit sparklers suddenly appeared as her golden throne surfaced from her watery kingdom below was a simple technical trick, she revealed. The sparklers and other fireworks would be lit and the whole scene filmed with Esther, her bathing beauty courtiers and her dais slowing sinking under the waves. When the sparklers reached the water, they were naturally extinguished. Played backwards, this same process gave the impression that the sparklers ignited as soon as they hit the air and stayed that way until the last frame (really the first one) was viewed by an ecstatic theatre of innocent movie fans.

In a way, I was sorry to have heard all these 'behind the camera' revelations. I thought it might spoil my future enjoyment of Esther Williams' enchanting films – rather like the first Christmas I discovered that Santa Claus didn't exist. I felt that somehow, the magic would go out of it all. How wrong could I be? Enjoying one of Esther's movies some time after our interview, I was completely overwhelmed by all the intricate aquatic choreography, fabulous sets and dazzling costumes. I was willingly transported into the realm of spectacular fantasy that Hollywood was so good at creating in those halcyon days of great motion pictures. The only new emotions I experienced were pride and affection for the wonderful star I'd had the privilege of meeting, plus admiration for this down-to-earth, charming and sincere woman, who handled all that fame without ever taking herself too seriously. Now that's what I call a real success story!

12. Don't Put Your Daughter on the Stage

Holding a passenger talent show is a tradition on many cruise ships. If the entertainment budget is particularly low, the cruise particularly long, or the crowd particularly enthusiastic, a cruise director may decide to organise such an evening. It is rather like the game show syndrome that has taken over television and is a popular way of filling out the entertainment schedule. Oddly enough, most people enjoy watching others 'strut their stuff' in public and admittedly a few of the participants have more gumption than talent. However, there are always a select few who have studied their art seriously and are genuinely pleasing to see on stage.

Over the years, I have presented everything from spoon and nose flute players to bird call imitators. During auditions I usually had an inkling about the entrant's chance of success and made up the running order accordingly. In order to retain the audience's interest, it is always important to start strong and end stronger. The middle can be filled with the others. A few arms may have to be twisted to get enough people to take part and at other times the auditions are painfully long, with the prospect of more passengers on the stage than in the audience.

On one such afternoon, the queue of perspective participants was so long that auditions were literally a matter of just signing up unless a run-through with the band was absolutely necessary. A lovely silver-haired grandmother from Germany, but living in Spain, decided that as the ship was international with large groups speaking five different languages, she would tell a 'cute little joke' in each of the languages. I was grateful to have someone on the roster who would appeal to all our guests and not just to the English-speakers.

That evening the show was going as well as could be expected and the ambiance was relaxed and friendly. When it was turn of the little German grandmother she was warmly greeted by the audience. For the next five minutes we were subjected to the 'bluest' material this side of a Las Vegas showroom. I sat stunned as I heard her slip fluently from one language to the other using every four-letter word known to the Tower of Babel. After each joke, when the only reaction was a collective gasp from those who had understood, she would say in the other languages, 'Oh, I guess the Germans, French or whatever, aren't in tonight.'

When she finally reached the fifth language, leaving that section of the audience as shocked and silent as the rest, I called out her name, helped her down from the stage, and then took the microphone. I said that the jury had unanimously decided to award the last contestant a special prize for her obvious fluency in languages. They would give her a multi-lingual dictionary as she had once again proven the old saying that one should not judge a book by its cover.

13. Action and Reaction

We spent one winter season on the *Ocean Islander*, a relatively comfortable and friendly ship of just 5,000 tons. We did seven-day cruises through the southern Caribbean, went up the Orinoco River in Venezuela, and then sailed back to Barbados. Although the weather was typically sunny and the seas normally calm, like clockwork, every Monday night at 8pm the ship would begin to make a movement that nauseated almost all the passengers and crew. I actually saw guests leave the captain's Welcome Aboard Cocktail Party on all fours. The ship didn't just pitch or roll, but undulated in the most unbearable corkscrewing motion.

As this natural phenomenon happened on a regular, weekly basis, it eventually took its toll on the nerves of the less sea-worthy workers on board. Every week the eyes of the crew would glance up at the clock mounted on the wall of the main dining room as the ominous hour of eight o'clock approached.

This Monday night terror became quite well known in the industry and certainly passengers who had travelled on the *Ocean Islander* did not quickly forget their reaction to Neptune's revenge.

A memorable incident happened during our end-of-cruise disembarkation in Barbados when I was stationed at the bottom of the gangway saying 'good-bye' to the guests. The port of Barbados is a man-made breakwater and not a natural harbour, so there is a constant ripple of water that makes moored ships rock gently back and forth. We were in between groups, so there was no one else around when a rather overweight American lady strolled up to me. Without an 'Excuse me' or 'How do you do?' she abruptly asked whether or not our ship was the *Ocean Islander*. When I confirmed that indeed it was, she immediately began to scream hysterically, flailing her arms wildly in the air. I was so dumbstruck that for a short time I could neither speak nor help the woman, who was obviously in great distress. When I finally spoke, all I could manage to say was, 'Madam, don't you like our ship?'

As I think back on it now, I realise how ridiculously like Terry Thomas I must have sounded. Once she stopped her lament and pointed down to her foot, I saw that due to the wave action in the harbour, the gangway had rolled over the tip of her shoe, just as I had pronounced the name of the ship. Luckily, only one toenail was broken as her running shoes were a bit longer than her foot. I have since forgotten what she looked like, but never forgotten this reaction to the *Ocean Islander* that many a crewmember would have been proud to call his own.

14. *From Hand to Mouth and Back Again*

Not everything that happens on a cruise ship is funny. The television show *Love Boat* did our industry a lot of good, but also gave a false impression of the crew's life on board. Sad things happen and many touching moments are experienced. One such incident took place in the Venezuelan jungle during one of our regular visits to Camp Canaima, a sort of outback resort based around a fresh water lagoon, not far from the famous Angel Falls.

A small jet was chartered by the cruise company and tickets sold at the outrageous price of US$175 per person. On the way up to Camp Canaima from Puerto Ordaz on the Orinoco River, the pilot flies through Devil's Canyon, past Angel Falls, the highest unbroken drop of any waterfall in the world. The water supplying the falls comes solely from melting snow and direct rainfall, so the grandeur of the falls decreases dramatically as the dry season advances. By the time of our final trip up to the camp, there was only a trickle plunging its way into the canyon far below, or as one tourist put it, 'Did we really pay 175 bucks just to see an Indian taking a 'whiz' off the top of that cliff?' He didn't realize how lucky he was, as often the canyon is so fogged in that pilots refuse to venture into it.

During one of our forays up to the jungle we had a large group of deaf German passengers travelling with us. People who have lost one of their senses tend to develop the others more acutely and the deaf often see things the rest of us miss. The group was promised a German-speaking guide for their canoe trip, unfortunately, he failed to show up and I was pressed into service as translator. The guide we were eventually given only spoke

Spanish and he was perched up at the very front of the canoe looking back towards us. I came next followed by the wife of one of the deaf gentlemen. She could hear and speak, but only in German, so we decided to run a relay operation to keep the passengers informed. Over the sound of the out-board motor, the guide shouted to me in Spanish. I turned around and shouted the German translation to the lady behind me, who signed the message to the passengers. After a few minutes, our communication lines were working smoothly in both directions and our German guests had a multitude of questions.

As I mentioned earlier, these aurally handicapped people didn't miss a trick. One of them signed an urgent question about a big ripple in the water 50 yards away from the boat. The alarmed look on the Venezuelan guide's face said it all. One of the famous anaconda water snakes was within striking distance. He had already explained how these creatures were so big that cutting them up was like sawing through a thick tree trunk. Special jumbo plates had to be used in restaurants, as the meat was too big for normal crockery. The list of sizeable animals these snakes could gobble up with ease was also rather shocking.

We all suddenly felt very vulnerable and painfully aware of the fragility of our canoe. The driver slowed down the motor to attract less attention to us, the local guide tamed his wild gesturing movements and I turned my head carefully to whisper my German translation to my neighbour. In spite of the dangerous situation, I had to laugh when I saw the German woman signing to her attentive audience. Her way of whispering was to crouch down and make the tiniest movements possible. The message got through 'loud and clear.' Without a single word being uttered, just using the creative visual language of the deaf, the German lady instantly turned her group into a mass of stone statues.

Mercifully, the anaconda was deprived of the international buffet lunch our canoe could have provided for him, but regardless of the imminent danger we had all been in, I would not have missed the experience for the world. I had been a small but vital link in the chain of communication for these lovely travellers whose handicap couldn't crush their indomitable spirit. I felt deeply grateful for all that life had given me and allowed me to share with others less fortunate.

cruising

15. Magic Moments?

In these days of high tech sophistication where just about everything can be explained or at least proven with a computer programme, I think it is truly wonderful to still be baffled by a simple magic trick. Whether a sleight of hand, card manipulation or a David Copperfield-style mega illusion, it is nice to think that certain things can still amaze and delight us. I'm all for the Magic Circle's strict rules banning their members from revealing how certain tricks and illusions are done because it robs all of us of those pleasant moments when reality is temporarily suspended or at least, stretched beyond all recognition.

That, in theory, is what is supposed to happen during a magic show. When tricks go wrong in a very obvious way, a wholly different kind of entertainment is produced often providing side-splitting laughs and unforgettable memories for those watching. Being a performer myself, I hate to laugh when things go wrong on stage for a fellow entertainer, but as long as no one is physically hurt, there's no harm in a discreet giggle from time to time. Here are a few 'magic' moments I have witnessed on a variety of cruise ships over the years:

One of the most baffling illusions is a magician's levitation of his partner. These are so convincing these days, that unless you are standing right next to or directly behind the magician, it is impossible to see how the trick is performed.

Not long ago, most cruise ship magicians used what I call the 'car jack' levitation. As no reputable illusionist uses this antiquated method today, I have no qualms at revealing how it was done. There would be a heavy platform on stage, to which, after much elaborate twirling about, the magician attached a solid vertical upright. This could be a broom, an ornate sword, or just a decorative metal pole. When the assistant arrived on stage, instead of her usual undersized G-string and sparkly bra, she would be covered in layers and layers of diaphanous chiffon, draped below her knees. She advanced zombie-like to the middle of the stage and with a quick flick of the magician's hand was rendered 'unconscious' as she leant against the pole jutting out from the platform's base.

Now the 'car jack' part came in. Instead of slowly rising from a vertical to a horizontal position as in today's magic shows, the magician scooped her legs up, raised them to a near 'three o'clock level' then lowered her back to a 'five o'clock' angle. Standing back, he presented his 'hypnotised' helper to the audience. The procedure was then repeated, but this time the helper was lifted to a 'one o'clock' position and then lowered back to the full horizontal 'three o'clock.' The music was played loud at these crucial points to drown out the sound of the mechanism. Anyone who has had the misfortune of changing a blown-out tyre on a car will recognise the movements described. They are the same as those used with a jack to raise or lower the car to remove the damaged wheel. For the assistant to rise up to and stay on any sort of non-vertical angle she had to have a long metal bar hidden under her flowing dress. This was slotted into the vertical pole and safely secured in place before the levitation began.

I have seen this trick performed flawlessly scores of times, but the one time it went disastrously wrong has stayed in my memory all these years. It was a well-known fact that the very tall magician in question had a drinking problem. It was also well known that his tiny wife/assistant was a woman capable of driving any man to drink, despite her diminutive size. Herein lays the foundation of our magical mishap. Whether he was so drunk that he forgot to secure her hidden metal bar to the fixed vertical one or whether he was trying to exact his revenge on her for years of nagging and bickering, we'll never know. All I can say is that when he lifted her to the 'one o'clock' position before lowering her into the final 'three o'clock' crowd pleasing spot, the force used to lift her, took her right off the vertical supporting bar. As she and her hidden metal bar hit the hard stage floor, a loud metal ringing was heard throughout the theatre. The tipsy illusionist was still standing there with his hands up in the air above his head, but he was no longer supporting anything more than his shame.

For what seemed ages, the downed zombie just lay there without moving. The audience remained absolutely motionless as they waited to see if she was even alive. Then, the unhinged assistant began to kick her legs about. She tried using her free arm and leg to right herself, but was prevented by the weight and size of the metal bar running down her side. Throughout this entire mini-drama, the stunned magician just stood there watching her grovel about on the floor like some elegantly dressed, beached octopus. By this point, realising that she wasn't injured, the audience and I were laughing so hard and I don't recall how she finally managed to get up. Our last sight was of her clumping hunchback-like towards the wings of the theatre, dragging the weighted foot behind her as she made hula-style movements with her arms. With every step she took, the metal bar that had betrayed her, rang out loudly as it struck the wooden boards of the stage.

Somehow the fact that the couple asked to disembark the following day did not surprise anyone…nor did the news of their impending divorce proceedings.

Some extremely clever magicians have made a career and a fortune out of ensuring their tricks go wrong on purpose. The British comic legend Tommy Cooper was one such performer and countless others have regularly enthralled audiences around the globe. In my first anecdote, the magician was a tall man and his assistant less than five feet. In this next tale, visual comedy plays as much a part as what went wrong in the tricks. This time the magician was the tiny one with an inordinately tall assistant. His stubby little legs had to support an over-developed barrel chest, whereas she became smaller as she got higher, with wide hips narrowing into child-like shoulders. On top of it all was a little round face surrounded by scads of voluminous auburn hair. They were French, but felt giving the assistant an Italian name added to the mysterious appeal of their act. Her real name was Françoise, but she became Francesca on stage.

I have often noticed that when one thing goes wrong, it is often the beginning of a series of errors and setbacks. There is an old French adage that says 'Trouble never arrives alone' and that was certainly true of the evening in which I saw the most calamitous magic show ever.

I have no recollection of the beginning of the show. It was only when four people were called up on stage from the audience that things started to go downhill very quickly. The idea of the trick was that after the magician blindfolded his assistant, the four people each gave him a small personal object that was placed inside one of four black velvet bags. Once filled, these smaller bags were put into a larger sack. At this juncture, the magician explained that he would randomly pull one of the four identical black velvet bags out of the sack and the blindfolded Francesca would use her extensive mental powers to magically see inside the small pouch and point to its rightful owner.

The four participants lined up opposite the mind reader, the drums rolled and the magician extracted one of the individual bags, holding it high for all to see.

'To whom do the contents of this bag belong, Francesca?' he intoned with a sepulchral voice.

She hesitated a second or two, then, ominously designated a burly lorry-driver type of man. The drums rolled again and on the cymbal crash, a woman's lipstick holder was held aloft. To check what it was, the bewildered magician took off the delicate lid and screwed up the bottom of the container, revealing the shocking pink lipstick the younger lady to his right was wearing. A few titters were heard around the room, but the mighty magician was not to be outdone so easily. He increased the volume of his already booming voice.

'Concentrate, Francesca!' he instructed. 'Now, to whom do the contents of this bag belong?'

With her slight slouch and fidgeting fingers, one could see that Francesca wasn't quite certain, but after a moment's pause, she pointed forcefully to the lipstick owner. The second bag was opened after the usual drum roll and cymbal crash to reveal a huge cigar still in its cellophane wrapper. The four contestants collectively looked at their feet as their smiles became too big to hide. The titters grew louder and longer, but the magician blindly lumbered on.

'That is incorrect as well. Please concentrate, Francesca,' he said pleadingly. 'Now to whom do the contents of this third bag belong?' he continued, trying desperately to sound enthusiastic.

Somehow Francesca still hadn't cottoned on to the fact that if she didn't change her tactics, she would be wrong yet again. Her long bony fingers sought out the third person in the line-up. It was an elderly lady with masses of grey hair and thick spectacles. Needless to say when the third bag was opened and displayed to the eager crowd, no one was surprised to find that a man's necktie had been attributed to the plump matron.

Why he insisted on carrying out this macabre professional suicide in public and why Francesca continued to choose the wrong person after three incorrect guesses is beyond comprehension, but continue they did.

'Now, Francesca, you must *really* concentrate this time. To whom do the contents of this fourth and final bag belong?' he queried.

Before he could finish his question, dear Francesca had already pointed to the only person that hadn't been chosen so far, so we all knew the outcome before it happened. The magician winced with pain as he removed a large lady's hair barrette from the little pouch and handed it to the person Francesca had indicated.

'Here, she says this is yours' whimpered the defeated magician handing the hair ornament to a man whose head was as bald as a baby's bottom. The audience erupted with laughter as Francesca, still blindfolded, was led into the wings by her humiliated partner. It's anyone's guess if he meant to have her bang into the wall on the way out or not.

After two burly stagehands carried a large steamer trunk onto the stage, followed by the magician and Francesca, the audience quieted down for the second half of the show. With a great flourish of hands and eloquent speech, our hero explained that he would handcuff his assistant, put her in a huge linen bag and then deposit the bundle inside the open trunk. A single heavy lock would be closed to make sure Francesca couldn't escape. A member of the audience was invited to the stage to verify the solidity of the trunk as well as the authenticity of the handcuffs and the lock. Everything was found to be in good order, so, on a round of applause, the volunteer returned to his seat and the show's final trick proceeded.

With considerable effort, the portly magician managed to clamber up on top of the trunk. He then bent down to draw up a thick cloth tube around him and the trunk. As it reached the level of his neck, he began to count, 'One.. two.. *three,*' pulling the cloth high above his head. Francesca who had replaced him on top of the trunk caught it. As she lowered the cloth tube, it became clear that the magician had disappeared and changed places with his newly freed assistant. Francesca's tight-fitting dress made her descent from the top of the trunk rather ungainly, but everyone was impressed that the trick had gone well after the earlier fiasco.

With upbeat music continuing to blare away in the background, Francesca remained immobile. If body language is as international as scientists would have us believe, then total panic was written loudly and clearly all over Francesca's face. She looked down at the heavy metal lock on the front of the trunk, and then back at her pocketless costume. As she bit hard into her bottom lip, her hands slowly searched her dress in vain for some place the key to the lock could be hidden. There was another look at the firmly closed trunk, then a quick peek down the bodice of her gown before glancing back towards the trunk. By this point, the band had run out of music, so the drummer started what was to become one of the longest drum rolls in the history of the theatre. It was now obvious to the audience that during their quick changeover, Francesca should have acquired the key to the lock from the magician. Who was at fault was now of little importance. What was urgent was getting the magician out of the trunk before he suffocated. With one final look of incredulity at the trunk that had completely ruined the trick, Francesca shuffled slowly off stage. Never once did she pick her feet up as she walked, she just sort of glided pathetically towards the wings.

The drummer was now sorry he had ever started his drum roll, but could find no justification for stopping it. A minute or two later, the two stocky stagehands entered clumsily onto the stage. A third man carrying a fire axe was quickly waved away by one of the others. Out of nowhere Francesca had suddenly reappeared and solemnly followed the coffin-like trunk off stage. It was not until a few sharp blows of the axe were heard, quickly followed by some rather spicy French expletives that the drummer finally hit the cymbal, signifying the end of the show.

How can you follow an act like that? It was my duty to bring this show officially to a close, so I walked to the centre of the stage and thanked everyone for attending the performance. My parting words were, 'Enjoy the rest of your evening, ladies and gentlemen. Oh, and when you turn in tonight, whatever you do, make sure don't leave your key in the lock on the outside of the door!'

My only regret is that Francesca and her magician husband never turned their disastrous evening into a professional gold mine. If they could have done on purpose what had inadvertently happened that night, they would be topping the bill at the most prestigious theatres on the planet. The rest of the world will never know what it has missed, but I certainly do!

16. From Black and White to Glorious Technicolor

I am an avid fan of the old black and white classics that thrilled the generations of my parents and grandparents. These were later introduced to me and my peers through the magic of the early 12-inch television sets, so it was especially exciting to meet and interview some of the greats of those bygone days.

I realise it is a childish delusion that many movie-goers suffer from, but I could not help thinking that the movie stars would be exactly like the persona they portrayed with such conviction on screen.

Although they were all heavier than in their heyday, the unmistakable aura of these true Hollywood legends was wholly intact. It was evident that plastic surgery and hair dyeing had been resorted to, in a desperate attempt to hang on to youth that was fleeting away faster than the passing of time.

I may sound like some old fuddy-duddy, but the stars it was my pleasure and honour to meet were of the old school, when a star was a star 24-hours a day. They dressed and acted like movieland royalty whenever they ventured outside their luxurious Beverly Hills mansions or Park Avenue penthouses. Their early studio training had not abandoned them, even though the film moguls who instilled in them the basic values of celluloid celebrity had long since gone to the 'big cinema in the sky.'

Whether that approach to life was right or wrong did not seem to matter. After all, none of us mortals wanted to see our film gods and goddesses looking like the rest of us. As the iconic diva Joan Crawford succinctly answered when asked why she was always so elegantly attired and made-up whenever she was seen in public, 'If you want see the 'girl next door,' then go next door.'

If you don't remember any of the movie stars included here, I suggest you go to your local DVD shop and pick up some of their classic films to discover the wonders you have missed. If it gives you a warm feeling inside just to read the names of those illustrious myths who are an integral part of our twentieth century culture, then you will be intrigued to see what kind of person lives behind the glamorous mask that inspired us and made us dream all those years ago up on the silver screen.

In Hollywood's Golden Age, actors were broken down into two groups - the stars and all the rest. Sub-groups of 'the rest' would include the stars' leading men and women, their co-stars and the long-suffering character actors and actresses of all descriptions. These unsung heroes played the nosey neighbours, the elderly matrons, the bratty siblings and the wisecracking sidekicks among countless other stereotypes. Once an actor was 'pigeon-holed' in both the public and studios' eyes, that is where he stayed if he wanted to continue to work in Hollywood. Even Lassie was never cast out of character, no rabid dogs or unseemly mongrel roles for her!

Eve Arden was one lady who made an entire career out of playing the fast-talking, self-assured assistant or best friend with a heart.

I was fortunate enough to travel with Miss Arden on the *Royal Odyssey*, a Greek-flagged ship sailing for an American company called the Royal Cruise Line. Since this beautiful vessel had started out as the *Shalom*, a post-war gift from the German government to the Israeli people, she was full of wonderful architectural gems. One was the plush cinema whose comfortable chairs and opulent stained glass wall panels made watching any film a delight. Seeing Eve Arden star opposite Ronald Reagan up on the giant screen in *The Voice of the Turtle* was a great thrill, especially as Reagan was America's president at the time.

My transatlantic crossing with Eve Arden was in 1987. I

remembered her from her television series *Our Miss Brooks* and her film appearances in *Stage Door*, opposite Ginger Rogers and Katherine Hepburn and *Cover Girl* starring Gene Kelly and Rita Hayworth. The younger people on board knew Eve from the smash hit film *Grease* with John Travolta and Olivia Newton John. Her acting was so well received by this new generation of moviegoers that she recreated her part for *Grease II* at the age of 70!

She looked amazingly well for a 77-year old woman when I met her, but I rarely saw her without her big, dark sunglasses, even inside the ship. She only removed them for her interview. She spoke candidly about President Reagan as a 'competent actor,' but also as someone who even in 1947 impressed her as being restless about moving out of films and into some other administrative or political role. Despite her imposing presence and almost tangible star quality, I could see unbearable pain and suffering in Eve's expressive eyes. No wonder she kept her dark glasses on throughout the cruise. In a moment of great vulnerability, this wonderful actress suddenly dropped her protective shield and told us how the spark had gone out of her life one day in 1984, when her beloved husband Brooks West died. For just a few seconds, the star was gone and there was just a lonely, grieving widow before us who found life empty and aimless without the one she loved by her side. So intense was this unspoken sorrow that we all just sat there, audience, interviewer and interviewee rendered silent by a feeling that we have all felt at the loss of someone special. To her credit, it was Eve, whose wisecracking characters were the backbone of her enviable career, who broke this reverential silence. She said, 'I'm sorry I'm going to have to cut this short, but if I don't get to a bathroom, there's going to be a very embarrassing situation to deal with!' With that, this lovely lady rose to her feet, bowed gently and exited toward the back of the room, accompanied by sincere and heartfelt applause.

I don't think that anyone who attended that special afternoon was at all surprised to read that Eve Arden passed away just three years later. In 1987 she had told us how the spark had gone out of her life with her husband's passing, but in 1990 it was her own unique spark was that was to be quietly extinguished. Thank goodness for films! Those of us left behind can continue to enjoy such wonderful talents as Eve's, long after they have moved on to other realms.

Joan Fontaine's celebrated rivalry with Olivia De Havilland, her equally famous sister, kept Hollywood gossip columnists in business long after they should have retired. Joan's classic film roles in *Rebecca, Gunga Din, The Constant Nymph* and *Suspicion* gave her an international notoriety that made her a household name and a recognisable personality. She was much sought after as a VIP guest by various cruise lines, if only to have her reveal more about her on-going feud with her sister than she had in her autobiography *No Bed of Roses*.

The company's directors had informed everyone working on board that Joan would be travelling as a passenger and that, under no circumstances, was she to be bothered in any way. The staff were wonderful the way they politely, but graciously 'ignored' her as per instructions and probably, her request. The other passengers were another matter entirely. It didn't take long for the news to spread through the relatively small ship that a Hollywood legend was travelling on board. Miss Fontaine had been out of the limelight for a few years, but was still a celebrity that our guests were anxious to ogle at, even if they didn't quite have the audacity to blatantly invade her privacy. There was, however, one notable fellow passenger who did have the desire and the gumption to force herself upon her.

Miss Fontaine was travelling with two other people - a lady of a similar age to herself and a younger man. As you can imagine, rumours were rife as to the identity and exact functions of her two travelling companions, especially the good-looking gentleman. Even though the term 'toy boy' hadn't been invented, the situation had long existed. The idea intrigued everyone on board and was talked about in hushed conversations around the vessel.

When a ship is in port and many of the passengers have chosen to eat ashore, it is a customary for the maître d' to organise lunch in an 'open sitting.' This means that instead of going to your regularly assigned table in the dining room, the waiters escort guests to one table at a time until it is full, then move on to the next and so on. Someone as important as Joan Fontaine would not be forced to sit with other passengers unless she expressly requested to do so. On this particular day, she must have asked to be seated as far away from the other guests as possible, because she was given a table in a small alcove off the main part of the restaurant.

Although Joan and her two friends were just three feet from where we were sitting, our conversation was constant and lively enough to provide a verbal curtain of discretion. I was on the far side of our long table and Joan was on the far side of hers, so I had an ideal view of this lovely star as she quietly, but animatedly chatted with her guests. Out of the corner of my eye, I noticed a tall, thin woman flapping about like an agitated goose at the entrance to the restaurant. She queued up with the other passengers, then when it was her turn, moved away to the very back of the line a few minutes later. Before long, my entire table was noticing her odd behaviour, which continued until she finally reached the head of the queue and swooped unaided into the dining room. We soon realised why she had hovered about for so long at the door, refusing to be escorted to a table like the others, because she 'innocently' chose to perch right beside Joan Fontaine's private table.

'Hello,' she said brightly as she pulled the empty fourth chair away from the table.

'I'm sorry, but you can't sit there; you see, we're a party of three,' explained Joan with a forced smile.

'And I'm a party of one,' returned our over-sized homing pigeon (or was she really a vulture?).

'You don't understand,' the star continued, 'we asked to be seated at a private table.'

'Oh, didn't the maître d' tell you? It's opening sitting today, so if you don't mind, I'll just stay here,' insisted our hungry bird of prey, as she drew her chair towards the table.

In the movies, just when all hope of saving the heroine is lost; the cavalry rides over the hill, trumpets blaring and sabres gleaming in the sun to rescue her out of the clutches of her enemy. As if on cue, that is exactly what the maître d' did, minus the trumpet and the sabre, of course. Before she could utter a word, the uninvited usurper was swiftly moved to another table at the other end of the dining room. The surprised look on her face as she was seated and handed a menu, all in one well-choreographed movement, was truly priceless.

Both my table and Joan's had been mesmerised by this brief, but entertaining show and afterwards my gaze inadvertently met that of Miss Fontaine. A broad smile swept over my face as I looked at the now empty fourth chair at her table. She too looked down at the vacant seat, returned my smile and lifted her wine glass in my direction. I lifted mine to her as we silently drank to one of the oldest sayings in the book: 'All's well that ends well!'

George Murphy is one of Hollywood's best-kept secrets. Good-looking, charming, a fine actor and one hell of a dancer, his tap dancing routines with Fred Astaire and Eleanor Powell in *Broadway Melody* of 1940 have not only stood the test of time, but rightly entered the dancing hall of fame for their intricacy, rhythmic excitement and panache. Having Senator Murphy on board and in our audience was a great thrill for Peter and me, especially as our show included a tribute to the great song and dance men of the past, and that most certainly included the fabulous George Murphy. We both noticed that he had taken a ringside seat and genuinely seemed to be enjoying our performance. That was a great compliment, but the next day when he came up to us as we were enjoying lunch with Anne Jeffreys, one of television's prettiest and classiest talents of the 1950s, to ask if we would have tea with him that afternoon, we were both reduced to tongue-tied idiocy. Somehow we managed to make him understand that we'd be delighted and honoured to join him for tea.

All I can remember from that wonderful afternoon with that extraordinary man was how sincere and unaffected he was. Here was someone who had filled movie theatres across the world for years thanks to his talent, who had been a very successful American senator from California and who, despite his on-going battle with throat cancer had remained the same loveable man who had been awarded a special honorary Oscar in 1950 by his peers who wished to show their great esteem for him and his contribution to their industry. Cancer may have turned his warm voice into a whisper and eventually silenced it completely, but the very thought of that true gentleman of show business is more than enough to brighten even the darkest day for me!

17. Super Bowl Blues

With all the modern technology now available, it is incomprehensible to some people that there are still areas of the world where you cannot see *CNN*.

The *Silver Wind* had been recently refitted with a very expensive television antenna that was only a few centimetres larger than the previous one, but was supposed to get the major satellite TV networks more easily. Unfortunately, in the southern corner of South America, there is almost a total blackout of these stations.

It was the weekend of the US Super Bowl and the ship was loaded with fanatic football fans from all over the United States. We received all sorts of threats of what they would do if we didn't somehow manage to show their favourite game of the year. As it happened, due to weather conditions, we were not only unable to get a television picture, but were unable to even pick up a radio broadcast of this all-important game. In the end the best we could do was to have the local port agent tape the game at one of the luxury hotels ashore where they had an enormous satellite dish big enough to pick up a relay signal from another Latin American country. The next morning I announced over the ship's loudspeaker system that in addition to having the results of the game, we also had a videotape of it, which would be broadcast continuously throughout the day and night on Channel 7. Such was the fervour of many of the guests that they cancelled their tours, ordered room service and ensconced themselves in their suites for a few hours of what turned out to be one of the most boring Super Bowl games in history.

Nevertheless, there were a few that decided to watch the game later in the day. One such 'gentleman' was waiting in the Card Room for me at 2.45pm, knowing that I would be there by 3.00pm to organise the afternoon bridge tournament. As I entered the room I saw him hunched down in a chair with his arms folded in anger, staring at the blank screen of the mega-sized television set. Hearing my arrival, he turned around to check who it was, then leant over to his wife and said in a loud whisper, 'here he comes.'

I always feel it's better to confront a situation rather than be manoeuvered into a disadvantageous position, so I went right up to him and asked if there was anything I could do for him. He answered in a voice loud enough for the whole ship to hear. He bellowed, 'I thought you said the goddamn Super Bowl was gonna be on TV all day long and not jest this morning.' I replied that that was indeed the case. 'Then why's the goddamn screen blank on the TV?' he shouted, gesturing victoriously at the obviously pictureless set. I mumbled something about the tape having to rewind itself, but as I approached it, I realised that the television had not even been switched on. As I pushed the on/off button, an enormous colour picture of football players instantly filled the screen. I then turned slowly for the 'coup de grâce.'

'You have to put the television on *first*, sir,' I said with as much sugar as I could manage without rotting my teeth in the process. His wife who had doubtless suffered the indignities of life with this ogre for well over 50 years was laughing like a fool, pounding her fist on the card table. He took one look at her; a last look at the television, then got up out of his chair and marched furiously towards the door. The last we heard from him for the rest of the trip was what he mumbled under his breath as he left the scene of his humiliating defeat. It was 'Goddamn Super Bowl!'

18. A Whale of a Time!

In their constant pursuit of new destinations, some adventure cruising companies have turned to the South Atlantic and Antarctica. There is the on-going dilemma of whether such tourism is beneficial to the planet, in that it makes people more aware of its fragility, or whether this pristine frozen continent should be off-bounds to all but the most serious scientific explorations. Whatever your own thoughts on the matter, I had the wonderful opportunity to spend a three month season travelling between Buenos Aires, Argentina and Punta Arenas, Chile. The 17-day cruise included stops in two of the Falkland Islands, dramatic sailing through the Straits of Magellan, an over-night stay in Ushuaia (Tierra del Fuego's capital and the southernmost city in the world), Patagonia and several days in Antarctica itself.

The Falklands War was not that distant a memory when we first arrived in Buenos Aires in 1989 and the eerie uneasiness we felt there was almost palpable in Port Stanley. The vivid television and newspaper images of that town were still emblazoned on everyone's mind as we walked quietly through the treeless streets. There were excursions out to the penguin colonies, but they were not nearly as interesting as the rock-hopper penguin families we visited on the private Falkland Island of West Point the following day. They literally ricocheted from one boulder to another as they descended the steep cliffs leading down to the swirling ocean below.

It was a regular pastime for the passengers on board *Ocean Princess* to watch out for the first iceberg and whale sighted as we headed toward Antarctica. A bottle of champagne was awarded to those whose sightings were confirmed by the bridge. A fabulous series of lectures and slideshows were presented by the famous Swedish explorer Lars Lindblad and his team of experts, preparing the passengers and staff for the wonders we were about to experience first hand.

By the time we reached the continent, we were navigating through entire seas full of enormous icebergs, not just the little splinters that had won the champagne for the adroit spotters earlier on in the cruise. The deep blues melted into crystal clear parts, which in turn bled into creamy whites. Each colour told a different tale – how much fresh water they contained, the amount of oxygen trapped inside or the lack of it. These floating ice islands were so incredibly big that it seemed quite unbelievable that most of the ice was still hidden below the surface of the unfathomable depths.

Passengers and crew were ferried ashore in small inflatable rafts called zodiacs. Everyone was given a bright red thermal jacket and hood to wear, over which the obligatory life vest was secured. With the freezing temperatures of the water, no human could have survived for more than a few short minutes in those icy waves. Two thoughts occurred to me when I first set foot on Antarctica. The first transported me back to my childhood and my small grade school classroom. I remember the teacher showing us the globe and explaining about the equator and the two hemispheres. I easily understood how we all walk upright, albeit at a slight angle, but how on earth did people from below the equator manage not to fall off into space? Surely everyone and everything that didn't become detached from the Earth's surface must be walking upside down? This still doesn't make any sense to me. My second thought was how much my lungs ached as I breathed. The air in Antarctica is so clear and pungent; it actually hurt to take deep breaths, at least for the first few minutes or so.

We had been given strict orders: no food could be taken ashore, no physical contact was permitted with any of the animals, no smoking even on the outer decks of the ship was allowed and no litter was to be left behind. The weather in Antarctica can change drastically in a matter of a few short minutes, so if the ship's whistle blew, everyone was expected to return immediately to the zodiac landing area. The occasional unexpected arrival of thick fog brought about soundings of the ship's foghorn. All the passengers and crew heeded their call to regroup and no untoward incidents occurred throughout the entire season.

During our exciting hours of cruising along the coast, an almost continuous flow of announcements from the bridge told us about the various species we could see on the port or starboard side of the vessel. Everyone had binoculars, so we all enjoyed unprecedented views of these incredible creatures. For some unknown reason, people tend to have an inexplicable affinity for whales. Is it their grace? Is it their size? Or is it some long forgotten link our forefathers had with these gentle giants of the deep? Whatever the reason, I saw many a face light up as a whale sidled up next to our zodiac. One flick of that mighty tail and we would have all been launched into the air like some oddly-shaped cannon fodder, but all the whales seemed to want was a loving caress on their remarkably smooth back.

One of the most violent scenes I have ever witnessed was when the bridge told us all to look to one side of the ship to see a leopard seal having his lunch. Naively, I thought he would be swallowing a fish or two like you see at the zoo or a marine park, but here was this majestic predator shaking the small penguin it had in its mouth with such force that the skin was literally detached from the body before the poor creature was ingested whole. Elephant seals, sea lions and all the other types of seals and penguins we observed were quite docile in comparison.

On the more gentle side, I was given the rare privilege to personally know a penguin from egg to adult. We had been told not to touch or move anything on shore, so on my first visit to the continent, I looked for a penguin's nest that had been built by an unmistakable landmark. I found one inside a sort of natural alcove. The mother penguin was sitting there on her nest like an expectant madonna. Occasionally I caught a glimpse of an eggshell as she shifted her weight to find a more comfortable position. I sat down a few feet away and spoke gibberish to her for a few minutes like you do to a human baby or kitten, telling her I would be back in exactly 17 days. As I headed back to the awaiting zodiac, I turned around several times to see if she was still watching me. Her gaze never left my retreating silhouette.

I kept my promise to my lovely black and white friend, practically skipping over to her grotto to extend my warmest greetings. If I said I saw a look of recognition in her eyes, you would think I was mad, but I truly believe the sight of this approaching giant covered in bright red cloth jogged her avian memory. I sat down opposite her, just as I had done during our first encounter. I could no longer see the big white egg that had created a sort of lumpy white pillow for her before, yet I couldn't see any sign of anything that had hatched either. My patience was rewarded because for just a fraction of a second, she rose a few inches from her nest, gave a sort of energetic quiver, and then regained her former position. It was just long enough for me to see that she had one small, grey baby under her expansive maternal belly. I was delighted and stayed chatting for another few minutes until I heard the ship's foghorn sounding and headed back to the landing beach. As before, my friend's eyes followed me until the thickening fog separated us like an unwanted curtain.

On my third visit, I wasn't quite sure what to expect. A renowned scientist travelling with us explained in one of his lectures that due to the extremely short summer, penguin babies had to double in size every day of their adolescent lives so they were fully grown when the harsh winter weather engulfed Antarctica once more. When I reached the nest this time, I saw my friend standing completely upright like a well-trained Prussian soldier. Beside her stood a fluffy grey sentinel, just as big as her, but not yet wearing the correct uniform of the penguin regiment. I was about to sit down when I heard some loud squawking behind me. A large male penguin was advancing up the beach in my direction. I got out of the way just in time. Feeding time is a messy business, but one that I wouldn't have missed for anything. I found a rock to sit on a bit further away than my usual perch near the nest and drank in this wonderful family scene. How quickly the baby had grown in so little time as compared with our slow and tortuous journey to maturity. Not wishing to disturb my friend as she and her family rested after their meal, I waved good-bye and winked in her direction. She cocked her head to one side and seemed to repeat my gesture. How wonderful nature is!

Seventeen days later, my heart was decidedly heavy as I made my way toward my friend's nest. There was a chilly nip in the air and the sun already had that wintry halo around it. The beach was awash with fully adult penguins with not any fluffy grey down in sight. They were all facing in the same direction. We had been told that when they were cold, penguins turned their black backs toward the sun to soak up the solar heat, whereas when they exposed their white bellies towards the sun, it was a sure sign that they needed to cool off. Their silky black backs were all facing the wan pallor of the sun, so they too instinctively knew winter was just a few days away.

I wondered if my friend would still be near her house and if she was, would I be able to distinguish her from all her seemingly identical neighbours. I stood in front of her little niche in the rock staring blankly for a minute or two. I remembered finding this little haven on the beach and seeing my friend's egg become a chick and that chick become a fuzzy 'teenager,' and how that awkward youngster had now become a full-fledged adult like all the others. Today, three penguins filled the alcove. I wanted to feel sure I was saying farewell to this little creature that had unexpectedly found a place in my heart. Without any warning, one member of the trio suddenly cocked her head and gently closed one eye. As I walked slowly back up the beach, I continued to turn around as I had done before, but this time, my friend continued to stare toward the darkening sky like all the other penguins. We had said 'good-bye' and in her natural wisdom she sensed that we each had to return to the lives our destinies had traced out for us. I can only speak for myself, but that brief and very special encounter gave me a greater love, respect and admiration for the natural world around me than all of Antarctica's majestic icebergs.

19. Going Straight to the Top

In life, so I have found, there are two types of people - competitors and the rest. This may seem a broad statement, but if you think about your own experiences you will eventually come to the same conclusion. Not all competitors are sore-headed sulky losers or aggressive winners, but there are those who get a 'buzz' pitting their own capacities against an opponent, human or otherwise, and those who really couldn't care less.

As a Cruise Director, you can imagine how many games I have organised over the past 24 years. Age and nationality are great influences. Latins participate whole-heartedly as if their very honour depended on it, whereas northern Europeans tend to be more reserved and are hesitant to make a fool of themselves in public. One is not better than the other, but as a game presenter, it is always a boost to have as many 'game-show types' on the floor as possible. The Italians are a gold mine when it comes to participation. As with their opera, football, or just everyday conversation, they play games with great gusto and panache.

On the *Daphne*, a Prestige Cruise Lines ship, I used to organise a 5.00pm 'Mega-Game' every afternoon. This was an ideal time, as we had usually left the port we had visited that day and it was still too early for most passengers to begin preparing for dinner. One of the most successful games was one where teams sent a representative to find a given item and returned it to the stage as quickly as possible. The first back was awarded 'X' number of points, the second a few points less, and so on until everyone had brought back the required object. We always tried to mix up the ages, genders and nationalities on each team to encourage guests to go beyond their normal circle of friends, thus creating a more jovial atmosphere on board throughout the cruise.

No matter how often I ran this game, something inevitably happened that shocked, surprised, or delighted me. One particular afternoon, a charming Austrian grandmother participated in the game. She was blonde, rather curvaceous, and accompanied by her new Italian husband, who was 25 years younger. Coming from a conservative country, this lady had definitely found Italy more in-tune with her carefree spirit than her homeland. The game was advancing well with all the teams garnering a more or less equal number of points while trying to outdo the other squads. Teams had brought to the stage everything from a set of false teeth to a squealing bar waitress still holding her tray of drinks - all to win a key ring or logo-infested sun visor.

The day's final request was for a woman's bra. No sooner had I announced the item to fetch than my Austro-Italian bombshell whipped off her tee shirt and bra in a single, well-rehearsed movement. Totally uninhibited, she reached forward to hand me what had been covering a considerable amount of 'terrain.' The audience reaction was decidedly mixed; genteel older ladies feigned outrage while the male population responded in an eruption of applause and whistles. Needless to say, *no-one* left the room. After the furore died down, I announced that we had our winning team for the afternoon and proceeded, completely unshaken, to distribute the day's first prize to the blonde grandmother's team. She was last in the line-up, so I had a little time to think before reaching her. With a steady voice, loud enough for all to hear, I said, 'Very resourceful, my dear, congratulations. For your outstanding team spirit, I award you two prizes, one for each ...hand!'

20. Blah, Blah, Blah…

Throughout my career, my ability to speak foreign languages has been a tremendous help to me and hopefully to the passengers and companies I have served. Although English is my mother tongue, I have been Cruise Director to Italian, French, German and Spanish-speakers plus a myriad of other nationalities, including, of course English-speakers. I truly enjoy studying other languages and cultures and have always tried to speak each language as clearly and accurately as possible. But even with the best intentions in the world, you cannot become completely fluent over night, so some mistakes are inevitable. When approached with the correct dose of humility and an ability to laugh at yourself, these foreign language foul-ups can make very entertaining anecdotes. I hope you find the following examples enjoyable to read and that they will encourage you to make your own international 'faux pas'.

Most major cruise lines issue their passengers with on-board credit cards. This not only allows the guests to leave all their hard currency in their cabins or even safely in their banks at home, but also lulls the cruiser into that unrealistic world of seemingly endless credit. With the facility of signing for everything from table wine, to shore excursions to a trip to the beauty salon, the final bill can often overwhelm even the most affluent of travellers.

It was during one of my very first 'Welcome Aboard' speeches in Italian in front of 1,200 passengers that I made one of my most memorable slip-ups. My talk had gone brilliantly up to the point where I pointed out the various uses of this passenger credit card. I explained that in addition to it serving as a ship's ID to be shown to the security officers at the gangway when going ashore or returning aboard, it could also be used like a normal credit card on land. Practically every service on the ship could be enjoyed just by presenting this little card and signing a receipt. The one major exception to this system, I emphasised, was in the casino, where only cash would be accepted.

At that point, the entire audience broke out in uncontrollable laughter. Now to me, there was absolutely nothing funny about having to use paper money in the ship's casino, but obviously 1,200 Italians thought it was the best joke they had heard in years. Being quite relaxed when addressing the passengers, I waited until the laughter had died down enough so that I could speak. I told my audience that quite evidently I had made a major mistake in my Italian explanation of the casino's gaming rules and asked for someone to please let me in on the joke. Everyone in the theatre just sort of 'looked the other way,' so one of my Italian cruise staff came up on the stage and whispered:

'You said the passengers can't use the ship's credit card in the 'casino.' In Italian, 'casino' is a whorehouse. You should have said 'casinó,' with the accent on the last syllable.'

Then, it was my turn to laugh. After a second or two, I put the microphone up to my mouth and said, 'Ladies and gentlemen, I do apologise for the mix up. To the best of my knowledge, we don't offer *that* kind of service on board, but if we did, it probably would be better to pay in cash anyway.'

Warm applause greeted my announcement and much affectionate teasing continued throughout the rest of that cruise as I was continually asked for directions to the 'casino'.

To people who only speak one language, hearing many others spoken must often sound like a series of unconnected grunts and groans. After one transatlantic crossing, some of my family had travelled up to New York to visit me on board and have lunch. In the middle of our meal, I was paged to go to the reception desk. I excused myself and went to see what the problem was. One of the new receptionists admitted she did not feel comfortable making a particular announcement over the ship's loudspeakers in the five languages required and asked if I could do it for her. I happily obliged, then returned to join my family in the restaurant.

One of my brothers had brought his little five-year old daughter with him and as we didn't often have the chance to spend time together, she insisted on sitting next to 'Uncle Gary.' Just as I was about to start to eat again, she stood up and cupped her hands around my ear and whispered conspiratorially,

'Uncle Gary, tell me the truth. When you just made that announcement in all those languages, you were really just making it all up, weren't you? I mean you were just saying, 'blah,blah,blah…right?' How can you answer such an innocent and adorable question?

'That's right,' I said, 'but let's just keep that our secret, ok?'

She smiled at me, then winked as she put her index finger up to her mouth to show me she would never breathe a word!

Sir Winston Churchill once succinctly described the many differences between the British version of English and its American counterpart. He said: 'The United States and the United Kingdom are two countries divided by a common language!' It's not just the varying regional accents on both sides of the Atlantic that create this kind of misapprehension, it is also the opposing meanings given to ordinary words that creates confusion at the least and chaos at the worst. This phenomenon is not just limited to the English language, it also exists in Spanish, among others, as you will see in the second and third of these three tales.

During one winter season in the Caribbean, an American magician had been hired to perform for an all-British group of passengers. The beginning of his show was all basically visual, so there were no comprehension problems as he moved smoothly from one trick to another. Once he felt he had warmed up his audience sufficiently, he decided to create a more intimate atmosphere by chatting with the guests. As he moved about the room talking continuously in his cordless microphone, he occasionally stopped in front of someone for a bit, then continued on to someone else. When he reached the stage, he held up the various pieces of jewellery he had taken unnoticed and asked the owners to join him on the stage to retrieve them. He cleverly used this brief pick-pocketing routine to select the two 'volunteers' - a husband and wife from London - he needed for his next illusion.

The idea of the trick was to have the couple sit down on what looked like identical metal folding chairs. One of the chairs had a small, battery-powered device that when activated, gave the person sitting on it a slight electrical shock. You can imagine how the explosive reactions of the 'electrocuted victim' brought peals of laughter from the audience. As it happened, the husband was given the 'safe' seat whereas his wife was seated on the pre-rigged one.

The magician began his patter in a calming and friendly tone, so the poor lady was anything but prepared for the small shock she suddenly felt. She leapt to her feet and let out a yell that would have woken the dead. The spectators fell about laughing. She was invited to take her seat once more by the magician who started to treat her as if she were delirious and imagining things. A minute or so later, another shock was given and the woman's initial reaction was repeated. Once again, the audience howled with laughter. Now the American magician took on a fictitious scolding tone, informing his unwitting participant that if she didn't behave herself correctly on stage, he would 'spank her on the fanny.' To Americans, that might sound innocuous enough; after all, it is what is said to children when they are naughty, but to the British ear, it is quite a shocking threat, especially when delivered in front of a packed theatre.

For those readers who are still confused, suffice to say that in the United States, 'fanny' is a cute word for one's backside; however, in the United Kingdom it is the part of the human anatomy that is unique to the female of the species.

The gasps of horror let out by the essentially British audience at this most inappropriate menace startled the magician. He knew he had been misunderstood, but wasn't sure which of his words had offended his spectators' sensitivities. He then repeated what he had said, but taking the lady by the arm, turned her around and mimed a spanking motion as he spoke. The embarrassed Cockney's husband shouted to him:

'No wonder you Yanks are having trouble with falling population numbers, you don't know one end from the other! That's her 'bum' you're walloping, not her fanny!'

The audience broke out in one great belly laugh, punctuated with enthusiastic applause. The magician recovered his wit quickly, thanked the man for his clear English-to-English translation, then turned to the lady and said, 'Madam, I apologise if I have offended you, and out of the kindness of your heart, all I ask now is that you just turn the other 'cheek'.' Laughter, clapping and wolf whistles greeted this request, and when the uproar finally died down, the trick continued and was rapidly brought to a happy conclusion. The intrepid performer's standing ovation proved what a strong bond there is between these two great nations 'divided by a common language.'

As I mentioned earlier, these linguistic differences are not only found in the English language, but in Spanish as well. The Spanish that is spoken in Latin America today is as far removed from its Iberian Peninsular origins as American English is from Mother England's way of speaking. During one of my seasons in South America, the ship's social hostess was an elegant lady from Naples, Italy. In addition to her native Italian, Carlotta also spoke good Spanish and English and had also learned the basics of French and Portuguese. Her language skills were very useful to me as Cruise Director because if I was busy in one lounge presenting a show, she could organise a game in another public room.

One evening after I'd finished the introductions to one of our ship's glamorous production shows, I thought I'd wander down to the other end of the ship to see how Carlotta's *Crazy Couples Game* was going. Long before I reached the lounge, I heard loud laughter coming from the open doors of the ballroom. As I quietly walked inside, I could see that she had reached the part of the contest where the male participants run and literally sweep a lady off her feet each time the music stops. At each round, there would be one lady fewer than the number of men on the dance floor, so the gentleman who didn't manage to lift a women in his arms, was eliminated.

Both Carlotta and I had learned our Spanish in Spain, so we kept giving each other quixotic looks every time the music stopped and she instructed her macho Argentine male contestants to 'cojela,' or 'pick her up.' Every time she said this, even the strongest of the men dropped the lady in his arms and everyone doubled over with laughter. There was obviously some misunderstanding because, as entertaining as the game is, it certainly did not warrant this excessive hilarity. I could see that Carlotta was becoming unsettled by this exaggerated response, thinking perhaps that these young South

Americans were making fun of her Italian accent. I discreetly went over to one of the men who had recently been eliminated from the game to ask what was so funny. He told me that in his country 'cojela' is like the 'F' word, a vulgar way of encouraging the men to copulate with their female partners. That this genteel Neapolitan social hostess was not only instructing these young men to realise their wildest fantasies, but also shouting loudly into the microphone ordering them to do so was as comical as the audience had thought it was.

I wasn't sure how to handle this delicate situation, but felt I must bring Carlotta's confusion and public humiliation to an end, so I walked over to her and whispered in her ear what the man from Buenos Aires had just told me. She instantly turned bright red, half from embarrassment, half from indignation. Her verbal reaction, however, surprised me. Instead of just graciously accepting the humour of the situation, she rebelled against it.

'Well, I don't agree with what I was just told,' she said adamantly into the microphone. 'All I know is that when I was living in Madrid, I often called the taxi company to send over one of their drivers to 'cojer' me, and they knew exactly what I meant,' she ended defiantly.

It is not difficult to imagine what followed. The room erupted in laughter. Some people were laughing so hard, they had tears streaming down their faces as they held their aching sides. At this point I felt Carlotta had more than done her bit for the evening's entertainment, so I gently took the microphone out of her hand.
'I'm quite certain they knew exactly what you meant in Spain, Carlotta,' I said, 'but if you say the same thing here in Argentina, you'd better be prepared for a very different kind of service!'

When everyone had finally calmed down enough to continue with the game, we made several attempts at picking up where we had left off, but each time the music stopped, the entire room shouted 'cojela!' and the uncontrollable laughter broke out once again. Realising that it was futile to keep on trying, we just distributed prizes to everyone left on the floor. The passengers spoke of little else for the rest of the cruise, so I was quite happy to see that they had left a little present for Carlotta at the reception when they disembarked. I was in the office as she opened up what she thought was a peace offering for all the good-natured teasing she had put up with since that fateful night. 'Oh, Madonna,' she sighed loudly as she pulled back the wrapping paper to reveal the box's contents. It was a small model taxi with the word 'cojela' carefully written on the car's roof!

While there are as many versions of French spoken around the world as there are of Spanish, this next anecdote deals more with the difficulty many foreigners experience when trying to speak the language of Molière with a good accent.

I was working on a small, but delightful little cruise ship that had quite an international mixture of passengers and crew on board. All the important announcements had to be made in five languages: French, Italian, Spanish, German and English and I was responsible for taking care of the majority of these broadcasts. For a few weeks, we had a Swiss-German excursions manager on board who insisted on doing them herself. It was evident that she had spent many years studying languages, but it was equally evident that she kept her thick, guttural accent in all of them. What she said was usually intelligible, but sometimes, comical. She had absolutely no sense of humour, and was incapable of accepting even the most delicately expressed criticism or correction.

I must admit, the first few times she made her tour departure announcements, I was too busy doing other things to really listen to what she said. By day three of the cruise, I cringed when she arrived at the French translation of her text. The main body of her message was usually fine, but instead of just saying it once, she said 'I repeat' in each language then reiterated the message. This worked fine in four of the five languages, but in French, her mispronunciation was quite amusing. 'I repeat' in French is 'Je répète' (ray-payt). What she said, however, was 'Je repète' (ruh-payt). The French verb 'péter' means 'to fart,' so instead of informing the passengers that she was going to repeat her announcement, she was telling them loud and clear that she was going to break wind again!

I felt it was my duty to bring this to her attention, but she would hear nothing of it. According to her, her French was flawless and it was my ears that needed examining. What can you do in such a predicament? I would have just let it go, knowing she was only with us for a short period, but when the French captain mentioned it during his weekly meeting with the ship's senior officers, I explained that I had already made one attempt at helping her and that was gruffly rebuffed.

'Leave it to me,' he stated. 'I have a sure-fire remedy for her.'

With that, the meeting was adjourned and I left the room wondering what he had in mind.

When the excursions announcements were made the following morning, we all waited with baited breath to see if the captain's secret formula would work or not. Whether on purpose or by chance, I'll never know, but that day, the French translation was kept until last. At the end of her first reading, instead of saying her habitual and unintentionally rude phrase in French, she said 'Encore une fois' which means 'One more time.' Muffled laughs and some spontaneous applause could be heard around the vessel, so the French guests must also have noticed her daily muddling of their language.

When I was certain she had gone ashore, I went into her office to ask her assistant what the captain had said or done to achieve such quick and complete success. She handed me a brief, typed letter.

It said, 'Dear Mademoiselle, while I commiserate with your ongoing digestive troubles, I do not think it wise to inform our French passengers of them, especially as you do so with alarming regularity over our public address system. Should this intestinal disturbance continue, please do not hesitate to contact the ship's medical officer. Best regards, the Captain.'

Talk about the 'winds of change'!

21. Ginger and Spice and Everything Nice

One of the most wonderful and special people that I have been privileged to call a friend was the legendary actress Ginger Rogers. We first met in 1979 when I was the principal singer at the famous Paris Lido and she was there to sign a contract to star in a television extravaganza, to be filmed at that prestigious location. We quickly became fast friends and remained in close contact until a series of strokes made it next to impossible for her to communicate.

Ginger was excited about Peter and me starting a whole new career on cruise ships and fully approved our decision since she had enjoyed her time as a VIP guest on the Holland America fleet. In 1985, Paquet's flagship *Mermoz* was making her first and only world cruise and Peter and I were lucky enough to be working on board. The original plan was for Ginger to join us for the last leg and then we'd all spend Christmas together at her home near Palm Springs, California. Her extensive work commitments meant that the dream of cruising together was impossible to realise, so it was decided that once Peter and I disembarked the *Mermoz* in Los Angeles, we would hire a car and drive out to the desert to spend Christmas with Ginger.

Driving in LA is a nightmare at the best of times, but around the holiday season, it is even worse. This traffic menace convinced me to choose the smallest car possible, which was a Honda Civic at the time. It had all the modern conveniences like air conditioning, stereo radio and cassette player, but its small size made me feel more comfortable in dealing with the six lane motorways that zigzag through that sprawling metropolis. It didn't take long to reach Palm Springs but we had some difficulty finding the

Thunderbird Country Club in Rancho Mirage. We rang Ginger who gave us very specific instructions and within minutes found ourselves at the entrance gates to the impressive compound within whose massive walls also lived the likes of President Ford, Frank Sinatra and Bob Hope.

There was a small hut on a concrete island with huge metal gates blocking the ways in and out. An armed guard sauntered out of this air conditioned cabin and gave our little Honda a look of such disdain that I wondered if he might use the pistol hanging from the belt around his waist to frighten us away. I rolled down the window and before he could tell us where the servants' entrance was, informed him that we were visiting Ginger Rogers. His half sneer, half snigger was full of self-importance, but when he exited his office for a second time, his demeanour had changed completely. He suddenly looked bewildered, chastised and humbled.

'Miss Rogers is sending someone over to pick you up,' he said. 'Please wait here.'

A minute or two later, we noticed a short, trim man walk out of a house not more than 100 yards away. He hopped into a Silver Cloud Rolls Royce and quickly reversed the beautiful car down a sloping driveway. Before we could count to ten, he was parked opposite us on the other side of the concrete island. After motioning us to lower the Honda's window, we were greeted by the most tanned face I have ever seen. His dark hair was slicked back and his ready smile boasted an inordinate amount of large white teeth.

'Hi,' he said, 'I'm Robert Kennedy. Just follow me.'

The metal gate swung up and we entered this inner sanctum of the very rich and famous. During the short drive over to Ginger's home, I wondered if we would feel comfortable spending Christmas with people who were so rich they drove a Rolls Royce

100 yards instead of walking it. Stepping out of the car, I looked briefly at our tiny Honda Civic parked next to the gigantic Rolls. It reminded me of a mother whale and her diminutive calf. This only heightened my anxiety. Robert Kennedy reintroduced himself, offered a very strong handshake and then flashed his luminous choppers at us once again. He knocked heavily on the big, white door and it swung open to reveal our dear friend Ginger Rogers. Her comfortable corduroy trousers, baggy knit sweater and simple black hair band bespoke the relaxing, casual atmosphere we had always felt whenever we were together. No ceremony, just good buddies enjoying each other's company.

'Dear ones, come in, come in. You must be exhausted after that long drive,' she said, grabbing each of us by the arm and ushering us into her spacious living room. 'Now, I've given the servants Christmas off, so who's going to help me in the kitchen?'

As my hand shot up to volunteer, I whispered to Peter, 'This is more like it!' His wink showed he felt the same way.

As Ginger and I sorted out lunch in the kitchen, I discovered that this Robert Kennedy was indeed one of the famous Kennedy cousins, but was not involved in politics. He was a show producer and had been working with Ginger to create a new musical for Broadway based on the life of Jimmy Durante. Ginger let it slip in a charmingly innocent way that in addition to their mutual business interests, they had been seeing each other romantically as well.

Our lunch and entire time at Ginger's was the stuff of dreams! We went to church with her for a very inspiring service. It was difficult not to keep thinking how the lady singing hymns in between us had entertained millions of fans worldwide with her memorable renditions of timeless George Gershwin and Irving Berlin tunes. Back at her house, Peter and I took turns holding the

Oscar she won in 1942 for her dramatic role in the film *Kitty Foyle*. We also saw official portraits of her taken with various American presidents. These photos were all lined up on her long mantelpiece. At the very end of this illustrious group was a small Polaroid snapshot of three friends. Upon closer inspection, it was a photo of Ginger flanked by Fred Astaire and Hermes Pan, their celebrated choreographer from their heydays as RKO's main attraction.

'This looks very recent. Is it?' I queried as I pointed to the photo in question.

'Yes. That was just a couple of weeks ago,' came Ginger's reply. 'You know, we take turns having dinner at each others' homes and that was Fred's turn,' she added wistfully.

'It's so obvious you're all such good friends,' I said, taking the picture in my hands.

'You know, all the hateful stories of how Fred and I supposedly don't like each other, well, anyone can see that it's just a lot of rubbish. We had separate lives and different interests outside the studio and there was a 12-year age difference... not to mention Fred's insanely jealous wife Phyllis. You know, those stories have followed us all throughout our careers and have really hurt us, but no one has ever managed to set the record straight. I hope they do some day. It would be a real load off my mind.'

As I was flying home from Costa Rica after yet another shipboard contract several years later, I was stunned to read in a newspaper that Ginger had died suddenly. I mentioned earlier that for the last few years of her life, it was difficult for her to speak or write after a debilitating series of strokes, so our contact with her had become one-way. Our letters and cards remained unanswered, although we know she greatly appreciated receiving them.

As a belated 'thank you' to one of Hollywood's greatest legends, let this short tribute to her and our cherished friendship be to finally 'set the record straight' as she would have wished: Fred and Ginger were warm friends and held each other in great esteem, and that's straight from the 'hoofer's' mouth!

22. Fly Me to the Moon

In the cruise industry, everyone is desperately trying to outdo everyone else. This phenomenon sometimes gives rise to fabulous new ideas, but just as often, it spawns real monsters. The trouble with instigating new ideas is that setting them up costs so much and a considerable amount of time must be allocated to see if they work or fail.

One particular 'innovation' I recall was the brainchild of the entertainment manager of a well esablished cruise line. He felt that he could get more mileage out of his entertainer package by having some of the artists follow a two-week on, two-week off policy during the summer season. By having one act do the last week of a fortnight cruise and the first week of the next, sending that artist home for the next two weeks while the replacement act performed the same 'end of one cruise, beginning of the next' segment, our boss felt he could double the entertainment package without doubling the number of people on his payroll.

In theory, the idea sounds like a stroke of genius, but in practical terms, it was a living nightmare. First of all, airline tickets had to be arranged and paid for. Even with the usual industry discounts, the bills mounted. Then, the middle-of-the-cruise ports were more often than not obscure places with irregular air links to civilisation. One example of this fiasco was when our artists' 'turnaround' port was Reykjavik, Iceland. Even at the height of the summer, Iceland does not enjoy constant good weather and calm seas. Ship's captains commonly skip a port due to high swells, fog or gale force winds. On one occasion just before we docked in Reykjavik, the wind was so strong that we arrived three hours late. For the passengers, this created a few shore excursion problems that were easily ironed out; but for us, the delay meant that we had missed the only flight back to continental Europe.

The local port agent was most helpful in arranging for a flight the following day, but had to pull quite a few strings to find us lodgings for the night. An international convention was going on in town and hotel rooms were at a premium. We ended up staying at the most expensive hotel in Reykjavik and in the presidential suite no less, since that was the only room available that night. We wined and dined and thoroughly enjoyed the luxurious surroundings the suite offered.

On rejoining the vessel two weeks later, we found out that, due to the same strong winds that made us three hours late for our arrival in Reykjavik, our replacements' plane had been delayed and they missed the ship. The vessel was heading towards Hammerfest, Norway, a two day sail, so that meant these artists were given the same 'presidential' treatment in Reykjavik as we had received, plus they had to be flown with their 100 kilos of magical equipment to Oslo, Bergen and Hammerfest in order to catch up with the ship. When you calculate all the airfares, hotel and food bills and inconvenience to the on-board staff trying to coordinate a most unreliable entertainment package, you can appreciate the disaster that was brewing.

As the season progressed, we missed the ship twice more. In Helsinki an unexpected air controllers' strike was called while we were waiting for our connecting flight to Finland at Stockholm airport. We were taken to the SAS Hotel where, once again only VIP rooms were available. As we prepared to fly to Leningrad (as it was still called at the time), a coup d'état was launched against Mikhail Gorbachev and the maritime facilities and airports closed down.

When the year's accounts were drawn up and the budget for entertainment was found to have astronomically surpassed what had been allotted, this new innovation was quickly dropped.

The shambolic inaugural cruise of the line's flagship after her expensive refit was talked about and fought over in law courts around the world for ages. Sadly that company was going through a real patch of bad luck. There were three major disasters in their fleet in the space of just a few months, leading many critics to blame the top executives for this unprecedented disorganisation. When asked about these allegations, a company spokesman humorously replied, 'Please don't call us disorganised. That's an insult to truly disorganised companies.'

23. When Adam Met Eve

When ship design became more and more important as a way of outdoing the competition, Croisières Paquet decided to do something really special with the *Mermoz's* midship swimming pool. Naval architects thought it might be entertaining for the ship's wealthiest passengers to dine while watching people swim in the pool. The walls surrounding the pool turned the rectangular first class dining room into a more intimate 'U' shape with a series of large portholes built into three sides of the pool. The idea of lithe mermaids and muscular Adonises gracefully gliding by these observation points was what sold this innovative proposal to the chairman of the board. Underwater lighting was to be installed to permit the well-heeled diners to enjoy this constant aquatic ballet even after night had fallen.

Too often there is a huge chasm between a sweet dream and cold reality and this concept was no exception. Instead of the firm, bronzed bodies the board of directors had been enticed to imagine behind the portholes, there was an almost non-stop parade of cellulite-ridden thighs and hairy, distended beer bellies passing by. Although the suggestive floodlights were placed in all four corners of the pool's flooring, a strongly worded message from Paquet's president stopped these illuminations from ever being used. At one point, there was even a rumour circulating that metal porthole covers were to be fitted to permanently block the unsavoury sights on the wet side of the plate-glass windows. For whatever reason, these 'iron curtains' were never welded in place and people quickly became used to this often-humorous display of human frailties.

The *Mermoz* was well known in the cruising industry for the excellent classical musicians it attracted and the young Bulgarian prodigy Boris Nedelchev easily met the requirements for an artistic booking on board. His dramatic and dynamic piano recitals were the talk of the cruise. No one dared arrive late for fear that there would be no places left in the theatre. On stage, Boris was intense and moody, but as soon as his tuxedo came off, a wild young lion cub was liberated. Although he was well over six feet tall, he was very childlike in everything he did and said. All he wanted to do was drink, have fun and drink some more. As long as he continued to give top-notch classical concerts, the ship's administrators left him alone. What caused his eventual downfall was not really his fault, at least I'd like to think what happened was done in complete innocence, but we'll never know for sure.

One evening after a particularly exciting programme of classical favourites, Boris felt he needed to unwind a bit. He and his girlfriend Anna changed out of their formal attire and went up to the late buffet to enjoy a well-deserved snack before turning in for the night. According to the head waiter, Boris ate like a starved stallion and drank like a thirsty sailor, but being the sturdy Balkan native he was, there was no apparent change in his composure, regardless of the huge quantities of red wine he had downed.

All these details were related to me during the urgent meeting held to discuss the ensuing 'scandal.' It would seem that after finishing at the buffet, he and his female companion decided to go for a swim to cool off under the stars. Most passengers refrained from swimming at night, but at that time, many cruise ships didn't cover their swimming pools; they were usually left full of water for the following day's early birds to enjoy. Had the amorous twosome taken bathing suits with them, there would not have been anything to report. The fact that they were both clad solely in what God had given them was where the trouble started. Yes, I did say 'started.'

The French are a very open-minded people as anyone who has ever visited the beaches of the Côte d'Azur knows, so a pair of bare bottoms or uncovered breasts would have brought nothing more than a casual or even an admiring glance or two. A fiery Bulgarian with several bottles of wine under his belt, a naked lady by his side and a dazzling moon up above is not just going for a leisurely paddle around a deserted pool. One thing quickly led to another and the couple was soon found to be making passionate, sub-aquatic love. With most of the underwater walls being made of thick, opaque concrete, it really was unfortunate that this ritual took place right on top of one of the glass portholes. First one pair of pale 'cheeks' was seen rhythmically rebounding off the window's surface, and then the duo would silently switch places, revealing a completely different bouncing backside.

By the time I was called up to intervene, a considerable crowd had formed at each of the six portholes. I heard everything from 'That's disgusting!' to 'How unhygienic' to 'Oh, yes! I remember it well!' The awkward part of my chore was not dealing with the collective peeping Toms in the first class restaurant; it was going up to the pool deck and removing Adam and Eve from their watery paradise. I tried to be as diplomatic as possible, requesting Boris and his girlfriend to leave the pool, but they were in a defiant mood. Instead of exiting as rapidly as possible, they slowly swam to each porthole and posed 'full frontal' for their audience. When they finally came out of the water, I handed each of them a towel and asked them to kindly return to their cabin, which they did with no further incident.

The spontaneous applause that greeted the moonlight bathers showed that, perhaps, the naval architects hadn't got it so wrong after all!

24. What a Load of Old Rubbish

Over the years, I worked on and off for a French travel company that organised round the world trips on *Concorde* and specialty cruises on a number of different vessels. One year they decided to charter *Norway*, Norwegian Cruise Line's vintage liner. This may seem an odd choice for French people, but the vessel had started out her life as the *France*, one of the most celebrated ships of the late 20th century and the travel company wanted to recreate the atmosphere of a more glamorous era. This grande dame of the sea seemed the ideal background for their project and to sweeten the pot, NCL had even agreed to temporarily re-baptise the ship *France*.

A series of cruises was programmed to tie in with the Cannes Film Festival in 1998 and we had international celebrities such as Charles Aznavour performing aboard. But the chance to climb the famous steps of the Festival Palace for a private showing of *Godzilla* was the reason most of the passengers had booked the cruise. The brochure also promised that a gala dinner would take place on board, with all of the great stars from the Cannes Festival in attendance.

Everything was going like clockwork. The passengers were happy, the weather was perfect and the atmosphere was electric with anticipation. Finally the day of the big event arrived. Breakfast was enjoyed by all in relative quiet, but just before lunchtime, what can only be described as a volcano of humanity erupted on board.

After carefully studying the daily programme, a small group of passengers had come to the conclusion that the chartering travel company had lied to them in their publicity literature. It was now clear that while the passengers were being ferried ashore to climb the famous steps of the Festival Palace and later attending the private showing of that year's film blockbuster, the likes of Sharon Stone and Martin Scorsese would be arriving on board an emptied ship to enjoy the fine cuisine of the gala dinner prepared by *Norway/France's* expert chefs.

This news spread like wildfire around the ship. Guests who had behaved in a very polite and civilised manner up to that point suddenly became a rioting crowd that literally took over control of the vessel. All the security guards and senior officers were called to 'red alert'. I was asked to intervene and liaise between the Norwegians who spoke only Norwegian and English and the charterers who spoke only French.

Since I had also been employed to present and often participate in the spectacular shows each evening, the passengers recognised me from my stage appearances. One particular group of hotheads had been searching the ship for the owners of the travel company, but as they had all taken refuge in an inside cabin somewhere in the bowels of the ship, the mutineers decided that they would take me hostage. One man was particularly vociferous, shaking his fist in my face. I told him and his companions that I completely understood their anger, but that no one from the French charter company would consider me worth defending. I was only a show presenter and interpreter and had no power to change anything. By slowly lowering his menacing fist from my face, I realised that he saw my point of view. I promised him that if he and his group gave me 15 minutes to locate and talk to the charterers, I would report back to him on what I found out. Everyone seemed to think this was reasonable and allowed me to exit from the tightly formed circle that had surrounded me for an excruciating ten minutes.

Once I was out of earshot, I used my walkie-talkie to communicate with the heads of the travel company. Basically, they had collectively decided to wash their hands of the whole affair and left the Norwegian captain and his officers to deal with the problem. I went up to the bridge and spoke to the captain, who had never seen anything like this second French Revolution in his quiet country of placid fjords and even more placid people. He said he had decided to cancel the gala evening and had called in the French police to help out.

As promised, I returned to the rioters and told them of the situation. By this point, a prominent lawyer had joined the group and convinced everyone that they should consider this a partial victory and sign up for a collective lawsuit against the charterers.

With the arrival of the police boats and helicopters, the crowds began to disperse and when questioned, no one had taken any violent action; suddenly they were all innocent observers. Even the people that the Norwegian security staff and I had accompanied to the ship's brig (yes, there was a brig on board!) said that they had only been trying to use the lunch buffet, which was why they had knives in their hands when they were apprehended.

Needless to say, the French and international press had a field day with this story. One of the most famous liners of her time being overrun with mutineers, whilst Hollywood's finest were ferried to the besieged ship made juicy reading for days and weeks to come. The paparazzi were all waiting on the quayside as the *ex-France* edged her way towards the dock. The disembarkation of the passengers went quickly and smoothly. Some of them couldn't wait to tell their personal stories to the waiting media, but journalists were there to interview one man and one man only: they wanted the 'big cheese' who had concocted the misleading brochure, filled the ship on this 'promise', then rented it out to the Cannes Festival organisers for their traditional gala dinner that officially marks the end of the

Festival. My staff on the dock radioed me on the bridge to say they were being hassled by the press to tell them when 'Mr. Big' was due to leave the vessel. They asked if I could give them any information to placate the newsmen. I went to the captain to see if he could shed any light on the matter. He gave me a wry smile as he answered: 'He requested to be disembarked first thing this morning on the barge that takes away the rubbish. Given his obvious qualifications to be on board that boat, I saw no reason to refuse him.'

25. Out of the Mouths of Babes

There is no doubt that entertainment on cruise ships has changed drastically over the last two decades. This is as true for everything that is organised to keep the adults busy and happy as it is for young cruisers under 18 years of age.

Quite some time go I had the privilege of working on the *Norway*, which before being bought by Norwegian Cruise Line from the French government, was the record-breaking liner the *France*. Although NCL had made some necessary alterations to many of the cabins and public rooms, in other areas it was still possible to see how this doyenne of the oceans looked during her heyday. The ship's theatre was the original showroom that had been reserved exclusively for first class passengers; one of the two restaurants was the very dining room in which these same elite travellers enjoyed sumptuous dishes prepared by a brigade of the finest chefs afloat. Even the hand-painted murals of the children's playroom were as fresh as the day they were created.

Enlarged photographs of youngsters cavorting in this same space lined the walls of what was now an administrative office. The toys and games were very simple and basic, but the smiles on the cherubic faces clearly showed the joy these youngsters felt as they sat on the back of a wooden rocking horse or held an artistic creation aloft with a paint-covered hand. On today's ultra-modern cruise ships, electronic games have replaced the heavy tin cars and curly-haired dolls played with by the children of the 1950s and 60s. No matter how sophisticated entertainment equipment becomes, children are still children and their refreshing honesty and directness of speech can bring a smile to even the most Scrooge-like adult.

Many cruise companies have both 'child-friendly' and 'adults only' vessels within their fleet. Just because someone chooses to sail on a ship solely for grown-ups doesn't mean they dislike young people; sometimes a short break away from the children or grandchildren is exactly what is needed for both parties to appreciate each other when the holiday at sea is over. I have worked on both types of ships and have to admit that I thoroughly enjoy having children around, especially during the festive period. I defy anyone not to smile when they see a long queue of three-to-six year olds holding hands and marching through the various lounges, dressed as pirates, or clowns, or wild animals. Whose eyes do not well up with emotion when these same youngsters stand on stage together dressed in their finery and sweetly sing *Away in the Manger* at the Christmas carol service?

On P&O Cruises' *Oriana* last summer, our youth entertainment team planned an American Diner event that was one of the highlights of the cruise for the children, their parents and other invited guests. As Cruise Director, I was always the happy recipient of a hand-painted invitation, delivered to my office by a delegation of charming post-boys and girls.

Their main play area would be decorated to resemble the inside of one of those iconic American eateries and all the children would be dressed to reflect their particular roles. The guests were greeted at the door by a very officious-looking maitre d' and then shown to one of the many tables that had been prepared with paper plates and plastic cutlery. Within seconds, a bevy of waiters and waitresses handed out menus and enthusiastically wrote down orders of pizza, guacamole and taco chips or a thick slice of chocolate cake.

No matter how expensive or technically advanced the toy, I

believe that most young children are happiest when they are given a few small props and encouraged to use their imagination to create the rest. Whether they are 'playing school' or helping to run a fictitious American diner on a British cruise ship, I find their whole-hearted participation delightful. I tried not to laugh when one little boy ran over to his parents as they arrived at the entrance to the playroom and shouted, 'Hurry up! We're playing restaurants...and we've got *real food!*'

Another over-zealous tot admonished his surprised guests when he told them they couldn't get up from the table until they had eaten everything on their plates.

It is common for cruise companies to use mascots for their young cruisers to rally around. These can be anything from an adorable dolphin to storybook characters like Noddy. These mascots are used as logos in cruise brochures, on the youth staff's uniforms and on any youth department printed material, but there are life-size versions as well. This means that one of the staff has to put on a heavy and often unbearably hot costume.

At P&O Cruises, Mr Bump and Noddy are joint mascots for the younger set on board. Noddy is definitely the more popular of the two and it is amusing to see how the children react to him. Some run to him, arms outstretched to receive a warm cuddle, whereas others hide behind the legs of their mum or dad, wondering how this well-loved friend became so big. The youth staff take it in turns to be Noddy and Mr Bump because it is not the most pleasant task on the roster, especially during outside events in the height of summer. Noddy may be 'inhabited' by a man one day and by a young lady the next. A cute comment I heard proves that nothing escapes the notice of children. A little boy tugged at the leg of his dad's pair of shorts and loudly declared that Noddy must have caught the mumps on his chest since the day before. The befuddled father took a long look at Noddy and then bent down to ask his son why he had come to that inexplicable diagnosis. 'Can't you see those two big bumps Noddy has today, Daddy? They are just like the ones I had on my face when I had the mumps!' How the poor father explained that one away I have no idea, but the following day Noddy was 100 percent better because Steve (not Sarah) was back on duty.

Parents travelling on cruises today find that their youngsters are put into manageable age groups with staff members looking after the needs of each level. Usually different rooms are dedicated to each group with the furnishings and games reflecting their specific interests. In the young teens' room, you tend to find beanbag style seats so that the young adults can lounge about as they challenge each other in computer games. Older teenagers seem to prefer a more structured room with lots of moveable chairs and tables so they can make up little cliques and talk their hearts out about the injustices of the world and how their parents don't understand them. This age group is always the most difficult to suss-out and to follow because the youngsters are at that rebellious stage when they see smoking and drinking as signs of maturity, especially when done in public.

On most ships with large numbers of teenagers, two night watchmen are hired to 'walk the beat' and make sure the under 18s are not behaving badly. These night monitors (usually one male and one female) are normally in their early 20s. Although we affectionately refer to them as 'Starskey and Hutch', they try to play down the policing side of their job, preferring to take a very low-key approach because after all, teenagers are paying passengers, as are their parents. I have heard stories of 12 and 13-year olds literally swallowing lit cigarettes rather than have any evidence available to show their parents. A large amount of Coca-Cola can quench more than just their thirst.

Underage drinking is one of the largest problems during the main holiday periods. If it gets out of hand, further behavioural problems may follow, so it is important to keep this teen 'badge of courage' in check at all costs. Night monitors usually know the tricks to expect and so remain at least one step ahead of the young passengers. At ports of call where alcohol can be bought in supermarkets, teenagers always try to sneak it back on board in different guises. The most ingenious method I heard about was when the teenagers poured vodka or gin into mineral water bottles and glibly carried them up the gangway. After this ruse was discovered, having our security staff insist that for public health on board, only unopened bottles of liquid would be allowed to enter the vessel subsequently thwarted it. Any opened containers would be replaced with sealed ones. The unwitting teens were left with their thirsty mouths hanging open when their 40° proof 'mineral water' was replaced by a much healthier beverage. Darker-coloured spirits hidden in tinted plastic bottles received the same treatment. Word quickly spread and new tactics were devised, discovered and dismantled. Keeping ahead of such clever young adults is not easy, but shows us that this latest generation will do just fine when their time comes to run the world because no obstacle seems to be too daunting for them. Their motto should be: 'Where there's a will, there are *several* ways!'

When I was a child everyone my age had read the book or seen the wonderful film *The Wizard of Oz*. After receiving a blow to the head during a tornado, the main character Dorothy is transported to the fictitious land of Oz.

Unbeknown to many people outside the gay community, this icon of children's literature was chosen as a sort of patron saint for them and on many cruise ships, informal meetings are announced in the daily activities programme as a 'Friends of Dorothy Get-together.' This same type of gathering is also arranged for other groups like the Free Masons, the Rotary Club and the Lions upon request. Other entities such as 'Alcoholics Anonymous' also prefer to use a sort of code name like 'Friends of Dr Bob and Bill W' as a discreet way of informing their members a get-together will take place.

On a cruise last winter, a lesbian couple asked for such a meeting be organised, so one of our lounges was set aside and the printed passengers' entertainment guide announced that 'All Friends of Dorothy are invited to enjoy a pre-dinner cocktail in the Viceroy Room at 6.00pm.'

As the daily programme for the following day is always distributed to the cabins the evening before, it was not until the next morning that Reception called and asked me to speak to an elderly lady who was quite upset about something printed in the ship's paper.

'I can't possibly pay for all those drinks,' she blurted out before even telling me who she was. I tried to calm her down and asked her name.

'My name is Dorothy Daniels and although I mentioned at the dinner table last night that I'd love to organise a small cocktail party for my tablemates before the end of the cruise, I never thought it would lead to this - an open invitation to the entire ship to have a drink at my expense!'

I had to summon all my strength not to laugh as I explained to her about the 'Friends of Dorothy'. There was a brief moment of silence on the other end of the line.

'In my day we called them 'Marys', she finally said. 'Why

couldn't they just have kept to that name and left me and my name alone?'

How do you answer that?

As cruising has moved on from a very elitist mode of travel in the 1950s to an extremely popular and democratic holiday option for just about everyone with more than tuppence in the bank, cruise lines have continued to develop their product, not only by trying to outdo each other, but more importantly, by giving all their passengers a wonderful floating vacation. There are very few holidays that can entertain so many diverse tastes, cultural differences and age groups as well as a cruise, so if you've not yet taken a cruise, what are you waiting for? If you have, just 'Carry on Cruising!'

26. All of Me

The lovely old *Royal Odyssey* had an attractive lounge at the very front of the main deck. This was called the Panorama Lounge because one wall of the oval shaped room was covered in floor-to-ceiling plate-glass windows. It was mostly used for cocktails and dancing, but occasionally, a classical concert or late night show was presented there because of its more intimate nature.

On one particular cruise, we had a talented ventriloquist on board as part of the evening entertainment. His two shows performed in the main venue had been so successful that one evening he was asked to do a shorter spot in the Panorama Lounge. As he was new to the company and wanted to continue to work with Royal Cruise Line, he happily agreed to this request. What he omitted to mention was that he had used all of his 'tried and true' material in his two appearances in the theatre, so had to invent something new for this special cabaret.

On the night of the show, the room was packed to the rafters, with people crowding around the two entrances, hoping to at least hear the witty 'dialogue' even if they could not see how much or how little the ventriloquist was moving his lips as his dummy 'spoke'. The first 15 minutes of this performance went swimmingly. It was all new material, but very much in the vein of what had enchanted the audiences at his earlier programmes. Why he wandered from that well-loved, well-beaten track is anyone's guess, but wander he did. When he announced that 'they' had almost reached the end of the show and would be finishing with one final 'duet', the genuine sighs of regret were audible beyond the confines of the lounge. He told his middle-aged spectators that the last song would be the evergreen *All of Me*. As the bright, swingy version of that old hit tune began, it quickly became clear that the dummy was to be the featured vocalist. What you must remember is that after two full-length main shows and 15-minutes of this late-night entertainment, the dummy had won over the hearts of even the most hardboiled members of the audience. He was the adorable, delightfully cheeky son or grandson they all wished was theirs.

For those who are not familiar with the lyrics of the song *All of Me*, they are an offer by the singer to the object of his love to take the various parts of his body because without her love, they are no longer any use to him.

The first part to be offered was the lips. As the lines 'take my lips, I want to lose them' were sung, the dummy's wooden lips fell away from his face. There was a general gasp heard around the room, but it was nothing compared to the audience's reaction to the words and corresponding loss of limbs to 'take my arms, I'll never use them!' What the ventriloquist thought would be a comical interpretation of this old musical standard ended up as a sordid mixture of public child abuse and the mutilation of a minor. As the macabre spectacle continued, you could feel the dissention growing in the room. I was once on the receiving end of a riot on the old *Norway* and likened the tension in the air to that never-to-be-repeated experience. Scowls now replaced the glowing faces of the earlier part of the show and a background of menacing chatter could be heard under the musical accompaniment.

The ventriloquist had opted to use recorded music instead of a live band, so this disastrous number could not be cut short to bring the brutal dismembering to a more rapid end. Whenever he wasn't busy helping the dummy to sing, he would smile wanly at the now hostile crowd. 'You took the part that once was my heart,' 'boing!' went the bright red heart as it popped from the puppet's hollow chest to a collective cry of anguish. On 'so why not take all of me?' what had not already dropped off the dummy's torso now dropped heavily onto the dance floor below with a series of thuds, bangs and thumps. A stunned silence filled the room as everyone waited for something to happen. Had even a short length of rope been available, there could have been the first shipboard lynching since the infamous mutiny on the *Bounty*, but luckily no such thing was to be found. The Assistant Cruise Director saved the day as he ran onto the stage shouting such a plethora of inanities that the audience began to laugh. Within a few seconds, the entertainer somehow managed to pack up his gear and leave the lounge without being detected. The only reminder of the evening's fiasco was one of the dummy's glass eyes that lay there in the centre of the stage staring accusingly at the people who had deserted him in his hour of need. To the superstitious Greek Captain, this single eyeball was a very bad omen indeed; the dreaded Greek 'evil eye' had been visited upon them and their vessel. The offending artist was disembarked the following day and a whole cleansing ritual was performed at the 'scene of the crime'.

That he was never hired by the Royal Cruise Line again did not surprise me, nor did the news that he had decided to work on land for the next few years!

27. Love Letters in the Sand

Most people would give their eye teeth to travel around the globe on a luxurious liner, but anyone who has ever done a world cruise as a passenger or even as a crew member will instantly recognise the condition described as 'cabin fever'. Oddly enough, the term doesn't really apply to your cabin, nor is there any noticeable change in your body temperature; it is very simply the claustrophobic feeling that sets in when you have spent too much time at sea. Everyone's reaction time is different, of course, but by the halfway point of this watery marathon, everyone had experienced at least one of the main symptoms of this maritime 'disease.'

A brilliant concert pianist named Yuri Boukoff was on board one of the legs of *Mermoz's* sole world cruise. His dazzling keyboard technique and choice of flamboyant repertoire made him a great favourite with all the passengers. To vary his piano recitals a bit, he asked some of the other entertainers with classical training to perform while he accompanied them. It was a wonderful idea and one that the passengers looked forward to as a highpoint of these musical events. I was asked to sing several solo arias and even a few duets with Yuri's wife, who had a lovely soprano voice. Yuri was a great bear of a man with massive hands and a massive personality. Everyone liked him, even the captain and some of his senior officers who were regular patrons of Yuri's recitals.

One day after a particularly intensive rehearsal, Yuri decided that we both were suffering from 'cabin fever' and in desperate need of a complete change of scenery. He asked me to put on a bathing suit and meet him at the floating platform used to embark and disembark the passengers using the shuttle boat service to go ashore to one of Indonesia's more remote islands. I thought I had been rather quick getting ready, but by the time I reached the pontoon, Yuri was already there waiting. He looked a bit peeved as he paced impatiently back and forth from one side to the other of the tiny platform.

'What's the matter?' I queried innocently.

'The bloody tender's just broken down, so we're stuck,' he answered, barely disguising his anger. 'Can you swim?' he blurted out.

'Why, yes, I can,' I replied not knowing where all this was leading.

'Well then, follow me,' he shouted as he dove nimbly off the pontoon and into the tropical water below. Such was his charisma or my foolhardiness, that before I could think this through, I felt the warm water engulfing me as I too, plunged over board.

I'm not a very good judge of distances, but we were probably a good half-mile off the coast. The waves helped us along as we headed towards what looked like a completely deserted beach. Eventually, we reached a lengthy stretch of the pristine, fine sand. For a few minutes we just laid there on our backs, soaking up the life-giving sunshine and laughing like two silly schoolboys who had decided not to attend classes that day. Rising to our feet, we saw a couple of children peering at us through the dense undergrowth that surrounded the palm trees lining the beach. There was a sort of rustling of leaves and breaking of twigs and then two tiny piglets ran out towards us as if in greeting. The two lads who had been spying on us from the safety of their thicket followed their pets onto the sand and started the most comical chase imaginable, with the pigs easily out-manoeuvring the boys. Out of luck more than skill, they finally caught their rebellious animals and ran back into the bushes without acknowledging our presence.

Yuri and I decided just to sit down and gaze out towards the horizon and our floating home. It seemed so insignificant against the endless expanse of azure seas.

Then, without any warning, we noticed long, dark shadows leaving us in unnatural and uncomfortable shade. Turning around slowly, we saw that a large semi-circle of local natives had silently joined us. It looked as if the population of a small village had quietly gathered to inspect these pale invaders of their paradise. They didn't look dangerous or carry any weapons, but still there were tens of them and only two of us should anything untoward ensue. What was obviously the chieftain or tribal elder stepped forward and bowed. By this time, we were both standing, so we bowed back, but this time just a little lower as a mark of respect. This small gesture seemed to please the old man as he bowed again, but even lower than we had. Somehow we Caucasians are not nearly as supple as many of our oriental brethren, but Yuri and I were intent on going one better, even if it meant an acute case of sciatica for the next week or two. Just as the chief was about to bow once more, Yuri suddenly stepped forward, extending his enormous hand. At first the chief took a swift step backwards, but then realised that this powerhouse of a man meant him no harm, so he put his tiny hand into the bear's claw and they shook. I was next in the hand-shaking ritual and this was then repeated many times over until the whole tribe had met these white curiosities.

Yuri and I could manage about ten different languages between us, but our hosts did not understand any of them. I tried to explain who we were and why we had come to their beach, but as I hadn't a clue what they were saying in response, I decided to use a big stick and draw pictures in the wet sand instead. This was an instant hit. Before long, several square yards of the beach were covered in a series of childish, but easily legible images. Such was the success of this 'ice-breaking' mutual entertainment that the chief motioned for us to follow him and his tribe towards a small path leading inland from the beach. By now, we knew we could trust these kind-natured people and happily joined the queue to see what lay hidden behind the lush foliage. Only a short distance from where we had landed was the most charming little grouping of huts that I have ever seen. They were all facing a central clearing, much like our older villages border on a village green. The chief looked solemnly at our faces to see our reaction. Sheer delight was written in our smiles and in our eyes. It was like an Indonesian fairy tale. A cluster of women of all ages appeared out of nowhere, carrying platters and jugs of various sizes and shapes. Somehow an impromptu feast had been prepared and we were the guests of honour.

After one of the most magical afternoons of my life I was suddenly seized with panic. *Mermoz* had just sounded her horn and both Yuri and I looked at each other in startled amazement. How could we both have been so completely lulled into believing this Garden of Eden could last? The worst part was we would have to swim back to the ship in the dark. I hadn't given any thought to hungry sharks or toothy barracudas when I made my way to the inviting shoreline earlier on, but now that the same waters were black as the night they reflected, I started to feel afraid. I needn't have worried because our most gracious hosts had thought of everything. While we were bowing and clasping hands warmly in thanks and farewell, the younger villagers were busily preparing an outrigger canoe on the beach for us. Yuri and I were invited to sit on a small wooden plank in the centre of the boat as one agile youth jumped in at the bow and another at the stern. The rest of the tribe pushed us off and enthusiastically waved us good-bye. A few of them were carrying lit torches which they used to ignite those placed at either end of the canoe to guide us safely back to our ship.

Whether the passengers informed the bridge or the other way around, every open deck of the *Mermoz* was lined with people, all curious to discover who was arriving in such splendour. Spontaneous applause greeted us as we descended from our beautifully crafted canoe. We bowed in humble thanks to our two escorts and stood on the pontoon waving until their torches disappeared in the gentle mist that had crept in over the lagoon. It was the perfect ending to the perfect day, that is until the officer of the watch informed us that the captain wanted to see us on the bridge right away.

As we anxiously made our way up to the captain's quarters, we began to wonder if we would be disembarked for breaching some archaic maritime convention with our carefree actions. The captain's glum look seemed to forebode the worst possible scenario. As he started to speak, inexplicably, he suddenly turned his back to us. He said, 'I suppose you already know why I called you both up here?' Without giving us half a chance to answer, he continued as he turned slowly to face us. 'It was just to say you lucky buggers!' he continued. 'I'd have given anything to have gone on that adventure with you today! And what a return to the ship! Yuri, this beats anything you can cook up at the piano. And now, gentlemen, how about a drink…that is if you're not above all that, now you're hobnobbing with local chieftains?'

We gladly accepted his offer of a drink and happily related the details of a most exciting afternoon spent with the 'people from Paradise'. I am still grateful to this day for those warmly treasured memories.

28. The Grande Dame of the Grand Canal

As a little boy, I remember watching an exciting television programme called *Voyage to the Bottom of the Sea.* The star who played the principal role of Admiral Nelson was the American actor Richard Basehardt. Little did I know at the time that some thirty years later and some 4,000 miles away, I would meet and become the close friend of his beautiful Italian wife, the extraordinary actress Valentina Cortese. For those who don't remember her, take a look at some of her great black and white classics from her Hollywood days: *Malaya* with Spencer Tracy and Jimmy Stewart, *House on Telegraph Hill* co-starring her husband Richard Basehardt and *The Barefoot Contessa* featuring Ava Gardner and Humphrey Bogart.

Valentina told me that when she refused the overt advances of Darrel Zanuck at a party one night, throwing her cocktail in his face, she knew her time in California was over. In Great Britain she thrilled audiences with her sensitive portrayal of the Italian mistress of an English composer in *The Glass Mountain.* She literally stole the picture from its star couple Dulcie Grey and Michael Dennison. The British critics enthusiastically wrote: 'First Garbo, then Dietrich, now…Cortese!' The French later awarded her their own 'Oscar' for her stellar performance in *La Nuit Américaine*, renamed *Day for Night* in English.

Although most people outside Italy knew her for her screen roles, her own countrymen revered her for her powerful stage performances, interpreting the classics under the skilful, yet firm hand of the legendary Giorgio Streller. She quickly became the First Lady of the Italian Theatre and has remained in that exalted position ever since. Her occasional poetry readings and theatrical recitals are always jam-packed, with many of Italy's VIPs vying for front row seats.

My first encounter with this phenomenal lady was in 1996 when I was working as Cruise Director and artist on board Costa Crociere's *Classica*. Our home port that summer was Venice. For anyone who has never sailed out of that gem of the Adriatic, it is one of the truly magical experiences in life. As the ship silently glides by some of the most recognised and venerated monuments in the western world, you have a bird's eye view of the intricate canal system and all the wondrous buildings that have lined the ancient waterways for centuries.

Through Peter, my former performing partner, a lunch date was set up with Valentina Cortese at the famous Harry's Bar on the Grand Canal. It is an intimate restaurant, with a very 1940s feel about it. Photographs of celebrities line the walls of the bar, with Ernest Hemingway receiving pride of place. In order to save time, Peter and I had taken a water taxi from the *Classica* to Harry's Bar and arrived exactly on time. As we entered the room, there sat Valentina, dressed entirely in cream, looking very much the diva she certainly is. Her 'trademark' turban was carefully tied in such a way that it was like a saintly halo surrounding a delicately sculptured face. When we reached her table, she embraced us fondly as though we had known her for a lifetime - indeed, after just a few minutes in her delightful company it seemed we had always known her.

She introduced us to her two companions; one, a dear friend from her youth in Milan, the other, the divine dancer Carla Fracci, La Scala's famous prima ballerina. To Italians, Carla is to dance what Valentina is to theatre. Both women have achieved and maintained the public's affection for more decades than seems possible from their exquisite faces and figures. That they were close friends was evident, each bragging affectionately about the other's accomplishments. I knew quite a bit about Valentina's fabulous career, so was interested to learn about Carla's performances opposite Nureyev and other greats of the ballet world.

All three ladies were curious about my work on cruise ships. They were close to tears when I related how, as the first cruise ship to visit the war-ravaged city of Dubrovnik after the fighting, people had lined the damaged walls of this magnificent city and waved us away with whatever piece of cloth they could find. The nuns had climbed the bell tower of their historical convent and rung the bells in answer to our ship's potent horns. Although the loud peals and strident blasts celebrated a first attempt at a return to life before the war, you could not help but be stirred by the whispered voices of the dead and maimed that they could not drown out.

Being an innate actress, Valentina easily understood the theatrical impact of this emotional scene. Having noted that all the cruise ships regularly leaving Venice sailed right by her home, she hesitantly suggested that she and Carla would wave to us from her balcony if the captain agreed to blow the ship's horns in greeting. Innocently, I agreed to this plan and we all clinked our glasses together to show a solemn pact had been made. Hugs and kisses and promises of future meetings abounded, then, Peter and I returned to the *Classica* to prepare our sail-away.

After I had changed into my uniform, I went to the ship's large amphitheatre to present my 'Welcome Aboard' speech before a captive audience of 1,220 Italian passengers. I explained the various facilities on offer, the excursion possibilities and all the entertainment options available throughout the cruise. Before finishing my introductory speech, I asked how many of my audience had heard of Valentina Cortese and Carla Fracci. Without exaggeration, just about every hand went up in response. When I told them that I had just had the pleasure of lunching with both of these Milanese divas, a mixture of applause, gasps and giggles met my declaration. As I continued my tale with unwavering conviction, I could feel, little by little, my credibility rising in the auditorium. By the end of my talk, when I told them we would be sailing directly in front of Valentina's house on the Giudecca, that both iconic stars would be waving to us from the main balcony and that I counted on every red-blooded Italian to be on deck with something to wave back with, the room erupted in one massive cheer.

My next duty was to go up to the bridge to inform the captain of this delightful surprise, before making the announcements over the loudspeaker system and describing the various points of interest we would be sailing by. Rather than blurt out the good news, I coyly asked if he had any objections to blowing the ship's horn as we reached the area of St. Mark's Square.

'I wouldn't have any personal objections,' he started dryly, 'but unless there is an emergency on board, it is quite illegal to do so.'

I couldn't believe what I had just heard. The captain noticed my sudden change of mood and asked what was wrong.

'I'm afraid I've already promised someone that you would toot the ship's horn as we sailed by their house. You see, sir, I had no idea it was against the law,' I ended pitifully.

'I'm sorry, but the law is the law,' said the master of the vessel with a note of finality in his voice.

'I wouldn't mind if it were just for me, but I've already told all the passengers to be out on deck to wave as we sailed by Valentina's house,' I continued, though I had already accepted defeat.

'Now, why would the passengers be interested in waving to your friend? They haven't a clue who she is,' he countered.

'With all due respect, sir, I'm sure they do. In addition to Valentina

Cortese, Carla Fracci will be there on the balcony as well and everyone in Italy knows them both,' I explained.

'You mean you know Valentina Cortese and Carla Fracci?' he queried incredulously.

'I had lunch with both of them at Harry's Bar today,' I replied quite simply.

'Well, that's a whole different matter. As a young cadet I was madly in love with Miss Cortese and as an Italian officer and gentleman, it is my duty to honour our beloved stars,' he pronounced with great flourish.

'I thought you said unless there was an emergency on board, it was illegal to sound the horn,' I said, genuinely confused by this complete and unexpected turnabout.

'I'm the master of this vessel,' he boomed, 'and if I wish to blow the ship's whistle, I shall blow the ship's whistle! In any case, any measures taken to keep our Cruise Director from committing suicide, professional or otherwise, would be justifiable in any court in the land,' he added, with an ironic smile on his face. This was a point I could not dispute as jumping over board had fleetingly crossed my mind rather than face a week of humiliating jeers and jokes from all the passengers.

'Now, just where does Miss Cortese live?' said the captain, drawing me out of my reverie. 'I'm not absolutely sure, sir...she just said it is a small white house right after the church by the Zitelle pier on the Giudecca. She and Carla will be on the balcony,' I answered, trying to remember any other details that might be important.

'That's great. We shouldn't have any trouble locating them then,' he said with confidence.

After my first scenic navigational announcement from the bridge, I went out onto the wing. Looking toward the aft of the ship, I could see that the Italians had heeded my advice and were all there along the railings, clutching their handkerchiefs, towels, or sweaters so that they could wave to their famous compatriots when the time came. I squinted my eyes as we neared the Giudecca, but could see no sign of anyone on any of the balconies that were visible from my vantage point. I decided to get a pair of binoculars to help me identify Valentina's house more easily. As I had many touristic announcements to make, I gave the field-glasses to Peter who was on the bridge enjoying the sail-away and also to have a better chance of seeing our lovely luncheon partners. In between my microphone commentaries, I looked out at Peter to see if he had sighted anything. His continual shrugging was starting to make me nervous, because we were only minutes from St. Mark's Square, which is just opposite the end of the Giudecca. Just when I started to despair, Peter came into the bridge and said he had spotted two ladies on a balcony hanging out their wash. The balcony did not belong to the small house Valentina had described, but to a luxurious and ornate palace. We both returned to the starboard wing of the bridge, this time with a pair of binoculars each. I quickly located the two laundry ladies he had seen, but as they had their backs to us, it was impossible to tell who they were. He was right though, a long, pink sheet had been attached to the white marble balcony they were standing on.

By now the captain was becoming a bit agitated and wanted to know if we had found the right house. I hemmed and hawed for a second, praying that the two washerwomen would turn around. The angels of the Giudecca must have taken pity on me because just then, they both spun around and began waving at our approaching ship.

'There they are, sir,' I said in a shaky voice. 'They seem to have unfurled a large sheet to help us locate them,' I continued. He put his own powerful binoculars up to his face and grinned like a child at Christmas.

'Giovanni, prepare to blow the ship's horn,' he ordered.

'Aye, aye, sir!' replied the perplexed seaman.

We could now see Valentina and Carla as they enthusiastically waved towards the *Classica*. The loud blasts of our horns broke the Venetian air like claps of thunder. The passengers were waving frantically, flash cameras were being held aloft to capture this exciting moment and spontaneous applause broke out all along the guardrails. Peter took pictures of the divas photographing us as we photographed them. It seemed they were as elated as all my Italian passengers. What a memorable sight and one that those lucky passengers will never forget. It became the favourite topic of conversation for the rest of the cruise.

The following day, *Classica* docked in Greece and I went ashore to ring Valentina to thank her for making so many people happy beyond belief.

'Darling,' she said, 'it was better than any opening night I've known in the theatre! So many people there and so much love pouring out of that ship.'

'Valentina, there's just one thing I didn't understand. Why did you have a pink sheet out on the balcony?' I asked.

'Well, I wanted you to see me, so I needed something big like a sheet. Since Gregory Peck had been using my house up until a few days ago, the only sheet that was still clean was the pink one, so that's what we had to use. But it was so creased, Carla and I were busy ironing it on the floor of the living room until the very last minute,' she explained with a girlish giggle. 'You know what was the funniest thing, though?' Valentina continued. 'In Italy, when a baby boy is born, a blue sheet is hung outside the house, and when a little girl arrives, a pink sheet is displayed. All of the passers-by shouted up to me, 'Congratulations, signora! And all the best to you and your little baby girl!' I told them that I'm the little newborn baby! Can't you hear the bells of heaven ringing for me?'

You can say what you like about the Italians, but I have never met people with such a wonderful zest for life who can make such a memorable moment out of something as simple as a pink sheet.

29. Is He or Isn't She?

In an effort to keep budgets low and variety high, many cruise lines have turned to Far Eastern and Eastern European countries to staff their ships. It is not unusual these days to find Hungarian musicians playing on British ships or Indonesian waitresses serving cocktails to Italian and French passengers. Although these hard-working crew members often have basic English skills, some very memorable language faux pas come up from time to time and are well worth remembering in an affectionate, not mocking, sort of way.

I have heard a Filipino band sing *Have Yourself a Merry Little Christmas* with sincere feeling, but unexpectedly rude lyrics. As these talented musicians tend to learn their repertoire by listening to CDs and not from printed sheet music, uncommon words easily get distorted as was the case with this well-loved holiday perennial. 'Here we are as in olden days, happy golden days of yore' came out: 'Here we are as in olden days, happy golden days, up yours!'

It was always a real treat talking to a mother and daughter acrobatic act from the former communist block. They were a mix of Ukrainian, Hungarian and Czechoslovakian heritage, but had a wonderful disregard for the inexplicable vagaries of the English language. I once asked directions from them to a small church perched high above one of the Norwegian fjords and was told to go up a certain road, 'pass water' and then go straight ahead. When I reached the waterfall they must have meant, my empty bladder let me down, so I couldn't follow their instructions! When trying to resolve a heated dispute between them and the Italian magician on board concerning the storing of their respective stage equipment, the mother of the duo complained that the magician kept putting his props in the 'back side,' when she intended to say 'backstage.'

My favourite funny incident happened in response to my questioning the mother about why her fingers were all black and blue on one hand. Her answer was quite contorted and drawn out, but well worth listening to, all the way to the end. She told me she had been suffering from severe constipation for the past few days and that the previous night during a rather bumpy sail in between ports, had awoken with sharp pains in the abdomen. She got out of bed, opened the closed bathroom door and went inside. 'Then,' she said with the most earnest look on her face, 'came the big movement!'

I just stared at her for a second completely dumbfounded, wondering why she had chosen to reveal this unnecessary and intimate detail about her digestive troubles when all I wanted to know was how she had bruised her fingers. She could tell by the perplexed look on my face that I hadn't followed her explanation, so she tried again.

'I open door to toilet, go inside, den come big wave and door close on hand. Ouch!' she cried, reliving the pain of the night before, all over again. 'Oh, that big movement,' I said, happy to have resolved the mystery. 'Vat odder big movement possible?' she queried, quite lost in the slippery subtleties of my mother tongue.

Another memorable verbal incident involved Nyta Doval, the exotic cabaret singer (mentioned in *Good Things Come in Small Packages* on page 23) and an inexperienced German show presenter. Nyta stood about six feet tall, had inordinately big hands and feet and the lowest contralto voice known to man. She could have been booked as a baritone, such was the vocal range of her lusty singing. Her brash masculine manner and poorly hidden cosmetic facial surgery all added fire to the rumour that was spreading around the ship that 'she' was in fact, a 'he.'

Nyta was quite a character. She told endless stories from her tumultuous past that were as impossible to believe as they were impossible to ignore. She must have been the unknown sister of the Brothers Grimm, such was the intensity and sinister aspect of many of these tall tales. Her warm heart and genuine dedication to animal welfare were what sealed a lasting friendship between us. I hesitated many times before finally informing Nyta about all the vicious gossip circulating around the vessel concerning her sexuality. I wanted to spare her the pain of hearing these unkind remarks from someone less interested in her well-being than I was. I expected any reaction but the one she had when I broke the news to her. She threw back her head and howled with laughter. Wiping a tear from her eye, she said at last, 'Oh, that's brilliant! Just what I wanted!'

'Are you mad?' I asked, seriously concerned that she hadn't fully understood what I had just told her.

'Darling, in this business and at my age, who cares what people are saying as long as they're still talking about me?' she replied.

'I see your point, but it's not very flattering what they're saying,' I countered.

'You just wait to see how full the theatre will be tonight, then, I'll slay them with my performance. Tomorrow, they'll all be begging for my autograph, you'll see,' she concluded.

That night, I presented and performed in a classical concert in one of the other lounges on the ship. Afraid it might run a bit late, I asked the German Assistant Cruise Director to present Nyta in the theatre for me. As it was, I made it to the back of the room just as Thomas arrived on stage. Because most of the passengers were German-speaking on that particular cruise, he began his introduction in his native language. Everything went beautifully. His English presentation was also going very smoothly until he reached his translation for the German word 'einmahlig' which means 'unique.'

I winced as he said: 'And now, ladies and gentlemen, please welcome the eunuch, Miss Nyta Doval!'

Hearing his words, a passenger in front of me held out her hand to her husband.

'You owe me £20,' she said. 'You bet she was a woman. Huh! What do men know about these things anyway?'

How treacherous is English, when by just emphasising the wrong syllable, 'unique' becomes 'eunuch'?

30. Are We There Yet?

Everyone has a favourite travel story to tell. It could involve departure delays, last minuite cancellations, horrendous hotel conditions or a vile mixture of all the above. Here is my own travel tale of woe in which I was required to join my ship in St Lucia. It took me quite a while before I could see the funny side of it, but I sincerely hope you will enjoy the humour of it straight away.

For the past 11 years I have lived in a charming little village nestled in the verdant Apennine Mountains, some 25 kilometres from Genoa, so it was only logical that my company should organise my departure from the city's Christopher Columbus airport. It is only a half-hour flight from Genoa to Milan, but I was made to take the 6.45am flight, so had to be at the airport at 5.45am, which meant leaving home at 4.45am and getting up at 4.00am. If that were the end of my sad travel tale, then I wouldn't be writing this story. This was only the first leg of a 48-hour nightmare. I had a five-hour layover at Milan-Malpensa, then, a two and a half hour flight to Schiphol Airport outside of Amsterdam. There, I was treated to a four-hour wait before embarking on an eight-hour flight to New York.

I was flying business class, so the extra space made my six foot one inch frame more comfortable. My grumbling stomach wasn't so lucky because my vegetarian meals never made it to the plane. They found some rather tasteless, over-cooked greens and some chewy yellow cheese for me to eat and I had countless whole wheat bread rolls to appease my hunger. Partly out of thirst, partly out of a real need to help wash down all of the rubbery cheese and doughy bread, I emptied a couple of glasses of some lovely red wine.

Needless to say, I slept like a baby the rest of the way to JFK.

After clearing American immigration and customs, I pushed my baggage trolley through the sliding glass doors and scrutinised the many hand-held notices, looking desperately for my name. It was nowhere to be found, so I waited, and waited and waited. Finally I decided to take a taxi to my hotel, so I had to get some dollars out of the automatic teller, then queue up at the taxi rank. When my turn eventually came, I handed the driver the name and location of my hotel. Ten minutes later, we had arrived and I once again queued up at the reception to check in.

'I'm sorry, sir, but we have no reservation under that name,' said the weary front desk clerk.

'Well, maybe it's under my company's name, or the agent's name,' I countered, handing him the paper my company had given me.

'No, I'm afraid there must be some misunderstanding,' he replied. 'You definitely don't have a room here.'

'Are there any other Hilton hotels nearby?' I queried.

'Yes, there are two others in the vicinity,' came the answer.

'Could you please check with them, then? I'm exhausted and really need to sleep,' I pleaded.

A few minutes later, I was in another taxi and heading to the correct Hilton Hotel. By the time I had checked in and reached my room, it was exactly midnight. As my flight to Barbados the following morning was scheduled for 7.00am, I had be back at JFK. by 5.00am and that meant getting up again at 4.00am, to ensure I was at the right terminal in time to go through all the security checks that are necessary these days. This was the next hurdle. My travel instructions just gave the number of the flight and its time of departure, but not the name of the airline. As the beginning of the code was JM, I deduced it was Jamaica Airways, but couldn't be sure until I reached the airport. Since there are so many terminals at JFK and the taxi driver hadn't a clue which airlines my electronic ticket voucher referred to, I took a chance and asked him to stay in the cab while I ran into the airport to verify my hunch. It turned out to be right, so after the check in and security rigmarole was over, I sat down at a deserted café and had a large coffee and a Danish pastry, because the breakfast buffet hadn't opened when I left my hotel that morning/night and my stomach was running on 'empty.'

My flight to Barbados went smoothly, but like the transatlantic flight, my vegetarian meals were at some other part of the planet, so I had to make do this time with spongy toast and lukewarm tea.

In accordance with Bajan law, before landing in Barbados the cabin had to be fogged with a most foul insecticide and upon arrival, a whole team of security agents rifled through the hand luggage and belongings of those of us continuing on to other destinations. With that over, we took off for St. Lucia and landed on that luxuriant island twenty minutes later.

I deplaned with everyone else, happy to be in a warm climate after so many hours of intense air conditioning. I was grateful to see that my luggage had followed me and felt certain that my luck had now changed. What a misconception that turned out to be!

As I reached the immigration officer's desk, he took my passport and transit form and studied it carefully. 'It says here you are embarking on your ship on the 10th, yet today is only the 9th. Where are you staying tonight?' he asked, looking at me over the top of his half-moon glasses.

'Oh, my company said the agent had all of that worked out,' I replied innocently.

'And what is the name of your agent?' he continued.

'Just a minute, I'll check on this travel itinerary my company gave me,' I replied breezily. I couldn't find the agent's name anywhere, nor the name of the hotel I was to stay at. The office had obviously forgotten to add this now vital data on the paper they had emailed.

'I'm afraid it's not written here,' I said as pleasantly as possible, 'but the agent should be waiting for me outside and he will have all the information you need.'

'This all sounds a bit fishy to me. You wait over there until I call you,' ordered the official as he motioned to one of the gun-carrying guards standing a few feet away.

Being taken to a far corner of the airport reception area by an armed policeman is the sort of thing they do to drug smugglers or gunrunners, so everyone was looking at me and shaking their heads as they pondered my lamentable fate. I sat there reading my book as placidly as I could until 30 minutes later when the immigration officer came over and informed me that he and his pistol-packing partner would accompany me to the meeting point outside to see if there was anyone to pick me up. My luggage was kept inside, also under armed surveillance. My heart sank, as I could see no one waiting with a placard with my name on it. Despite the humid heat, I broke out in a very cold sweat. It was no longer a slight oversight by the girls in the office, I could be facing a prison sentence. Suddenly, the officer said, 'Isn't that the name of the company you said you work for?' pointing towards a small notice.

'Yes! Yes it is!' I answered gingerly.

The three of us approached the man with the sign, but wouldn't you know it? My name was not on his list! By now, my shirt looked like I had just taken a shower, fully clothed, but I wasn't going to give in that easily. I presented my official embarkation papers as Cruise Director. That seemed to do the trick and the agent quickly tried to regain lost ground.

'It must be some sort of administrative mix-up,' he explained, forcing a nervous little laugh. 'You know what these young secretaries are like these days. Better if you do everything yourself,' he ventured.

'Well, if I release this man into your custody, you'll be responsible for whatever he does until he boards his ship tomorrow, and you'll have to sign the paperwork to show you mean business,' the officer said menacingly. The agent shot a quick glance at me to see if I looked like the type that would do anything that could land his sorry soul in gaol, and I guess he liked what he saw because he agreed to the terms offered.

A few phone calls later and I was bundled into a spacious taxi and began a 90-minute taxi ride across some of the bumpiest and most potholed roads in the western hemisphere. I had been jostled about so much that I was feeling quite nauseous as I exited the taxi in front of my hotel. There was just one room left and it had been held for me. A young bellboy helped me with my cases across manicured lawns and inviting swimming pools and up two flights of steps to my room. As we entered the room, I burst out laughing. This really was the icing on the cake. The entire room had been decorated as a bridal suite with festoons, ribbons and flower garlands hanging from every part of the ceiling and the canopy over the bed.

'I think we'd better call the reception,' suggested the astute bellboy. Once he had finished his brief telephone conversation in a mumbled sort of creole dialect, he turned to me and said, 'It's ok. The bride and groom had a big fight at the church, so they won't be needing this room tonight. Do you want me to help you take down the decorations?'

'No,' I answered, wearily, 'I'm so tired after all this travel that if I don't wake up tomorrow morning, they'll do nicely for my lying in state.' His eyes grew as big as saucers as he quickly made the sign of the cross. I handed him a few dollars and thanked him for his help. He bowed his way out of the room and made one more sign of the cross before closing the door behind him.

It was all I could do to get out of my clothes and into my marital bed for one. I did not stir for 12 hours. When I opened my eyes the following morning, I wasn't quite sure where I was. All the bridal decorations were still there, my bags were still there, but I could distinctly smell the wonderful aroma of freshly brewed coffee. I looked over toward the large round table by the balcony door and saw that someone must have entered the room while I was sleeping because there was a big tray piled high with breakfast fare. I staggered over to the balcony door, threw open the curtains, then plonked myself down in one of the bamboo chairs. There was a small card on top of the plastic plate cover. It was from my company's travel department. It said: 'Sorry for the slight mix-up with the hotel. Hope the rest of your trip was enjoyable.' I was too groggy to laugh or to cry, so just poured out a hot cup of coffee and absent-mindedly buttered my toast as I looked out at the glorious morning sunshine. 'Yes,' I answered to no-one but the birds on my balcony, 'the rest of my trip was fantastic. Thanks for asking!'

31. Traffic Jams at Sea?

No one would believe you if you said you had been run-over during your latest cruise, especially when you explained that it happened on board! Only those who have travelled on a cruise ship with a large percentage of elderly passengers can imagine this dilemma. Years ago, disabled people rarely took a cruise and those who did usually took a companion to take care of them. Today, most liners have specially built cabins for handicapped cruisers and access ramps into and out of the restaurants, theatres and other venues throughout the ship. Of course people with disabilities should have as much right to go cruising as their healthier or hardier fellow tourists. The problem that this improved accessibility has created is a lack of space for all the wheelchairs and battery-powered buggies that now speed along the once tranquil corridors of today's cruise ships.

Although some people still use the traditional wheelchairs that either need someone to push them or require the user to spin the wheels on their own, most cruise passengers are affluent enough to buy the electric models that can back-up almost as quickly as they can move forward. The mini golf-style carts, however, are the real menace as they go much faster and take up a lot more room because they cannot be folded up like many wheelchairs.

Naval architects have responded to international laws requiring today's cruising fleets to be more user-friendly for those with disabilities, but none of them has responded to the need for a floating parking lot for these modern means of locomotion, nor thought about posting speed limits along the narrow hallways of the vessels they design. I can't foresee anything like speed bumps, cameras or traffic lights being installed in the near future, but can remember one cruise in particular when they would have been useful. A long-suffering group of younger passengers became fed up with having to wend their way through the dozens of handicap vehicles that blocked every entrance and exit to the ship's main theatre night after night. This unintentional obstacle course was quite illegal, of course, as it impeded the evacuation of passengers and crew in case of an emergency, but no matter how many announcements were made over the ship's loudspeakers or how many notices were printed in the ship's daily newspaper, the users of this transportation took no heed and continued to park wherever they felt like it.

We never found out who it was, but their subtle guerrilla tactics were more effective than any of the toned-down measures taken by the cruise lines. After one of the evening shows, those who had abandoned their vehicles in an unsafe place found an authentic-looking traffic violation ticket attached. It warned the owner that if he or she were to infringe upon the safety of the other passengers again, further action would be taken. Some of the offenders just laughed, others tore up the tickets in poorly concealed rage, while a third group looked quite worried indeed.

The next night it was obvious that many had decided to 'obey the law' and had parked more considerately. Others had tacitly opted to take up this challenge to their self-attributed rights and left their buggies in blatantly controversial areas.

Who did it, how it was done, or when it was done has always remained a mystery despite some obvious suspects, but the astonished looks on the faces of the guilty when they found their get-away cars had been clamped were truly priceless. It was absolute torture trying not to laugh when they sought me out to complain. Calmly showing them the very prominent notice in the ship's paper asking buggy users to leave their little cars only in designated areas just made them angrier. Those who had taken heed of the written warning the previous evening provocatively honked their little horns as they blithely drove past their more defiant compatriots. After a few minutes of shouted threats, pitiful pleading and some rare, but very welcome apologising, the ship's carpenter was called. The chains the vigilante traffic wardens had used were so thick that a special metal saw had to be employed to free the impounded buggies.

Needless to say, for the rest of the cruise our reformed 'criminals' stayed on the right side of the law and we all lived happily ever after … at least until the next lot of buggy-riding passengers embarked!

32. Hokus-Pokus

Many traditional-style magicians who work on cruise ships still use animals in their acts. Some have small doves, whereas others prefer bigger animals like rabbits, ducks and lap dogs. Up to a few years ago, I hadn't had any contact with rabbits, so I was unaware of how clever, affectionate and loveable they are.

When the resident magician had to leave the ship for an unexpected family bereavement, he was in a quandary as to what to do with his rabbit and doves. Even in those pre-9/11 days, a lot of official paperwork had to be furnished before any live animals were legally allowed to embark. He was anxious to find a solution that would allow his magical menagerie to stay on board during his temporary absence from the vessel. Knowing that my performing partner and I are both animal lovers, he approached us to see if we would agree to 'babysit' for two weeks. Knowing how much he had already suffered at the loss of a loved-one and that he really cared for these lovely little creatures, we readily said we'd be more than happy to look after them. He gave us some brief instructions, several packets of bird seed and rabbit pellets as well as the animals' health certificates in case there were any problems with local customs officials during the upcoming fortnight. It was truly touching to see how he lovingly took each one of them in his arms and gently kissed them before he headed out of our cabin. He gave each of us a big bear hug and tried to thank us for being so willing to come to his aid, but the words stuck in his throat. I could have sworn I saw him brush a tear from his eye as he quietly closed our cabin door.

Our small but well-designed bathroom had a retractable cord that stretched the width of the shower to dry hand washing. The doves loved perching on it all in a row, just as their wild cousins do on telephone wires around the globe. By lining the bottom of the shower with newspapers, the birds became easy to manage. Hokus the rabbit was another matter all together. Our magician friend said that he tended to leave Hokus in his spacious cage except when he was in the cabin; then, he would allow this magical bunny to stretch his legs a bit. It may sound cruel to leave a rabbit in a cage for hours at a time, but Mike the magician explained that rabbits will gnaw at everything, especially plastic and rubber. With so many electrical wires trailing along the floor, he was afraid Hokus might bite into one and electrocute himself, so unless he was in the cabin to keep an eye on him, Hokus was safer tucked away in his cage.

With two adoring babysitters to look after him, Hokus got lots of cuddles and attention. Crisp lettuce leaves and fresh carrot sticks were snuck down to him from the lunch buffets on a daily basis. Although I fully understood Mike's concern about low-lying electrical wires within Hokus' reach, our cabin had alternative sockets everywhere, so this was not an issue. When we discovered that if we left the bathroom door open, Hokus would happily do his 'business' on the papers lining the shower floor, we decided that he could have free rein of the entire cabin. We informed our cabin steward about this decision and he had no objections; on the contrary, he willingly became another adoptive uncle to this adorable rabbit.

After a few days of total liberty, I noticed that each time we left the cabin, Hokus would agitatedly run around in a big circle anti-clockwise, yet when we returned, he made a figure of eight shape as he scampered excitedly across the carpet. During the two weeks we looked after him, he never changed this pattern of showing his sadness at our departures and joy at our arrivals.

One of the most touching ways Hokus showed his affection

happened shortly after he first arrived in our cabin as a lodger. In the middle of the night, I turned over in my sleep and touched something warm and furry. As my cats at home have always climbed in bed with me whenever they were cold or wanted company, this didn't startle me, in fact, I just instinctively put my arms around Hokus and we slept on peacefully until the alarm went off the next morning. It wasn't until I opened my eyes that I realised where I was and that I wasn't cuddling a cat, but a precious little rabbit. My first thought was to check the bedding to see if he'd had an 'accident' during the night, but no, he had been a good boy. For the rest of his time with us, Hokus assumed his nocturnal rights were now extended to sleeping with either Peter or me.

The only damage he did to the cabin was really quite sweet and certainly not vandalistic in the least. Whether it was to sharpen his teeth or whether he was just expressing an artistic urge, he had carefully nibbled the bottom of our shower curtain, leaving a lace-like pattern all the way along its hem. The result was quite decorative, and as we only discovered this rabbit masterpiece after Mike had taken Hokus back to his own cabin, we decided just to leave it that way in memory of a very happy fortnight with a very extraordinary little creature.

As incredible as it seems, for the rest of Mike's time on board, Hokus never forgot his two loving uncles and would dart out of Mike's cabin and head straight for ours whenever the door was open. When Mike first saw his prize rabbit scooting out of the cabin, he was frightened, thinking Hokus would get lost around the ship, but as soon as he saw where his rabbit was heading, he took it as a sign that Hokus had been well looked after and just wanted a little spoiling from time to time.

Our main worry was that we had been too lenient with Hokus by allowing him to go wherever he wanted and the idea of him being locked up in a cage really upset us. I decided I'd have to talk to Mike about this and see what could be done. One morning I went to

Mike's cabin and knocked on the door.

'The door's unlocked,' came the answer.

I slowly opened the door and shouted, 'Mike, it's me. Can I come in?'

'Of course you can,' he replied. As soon as I was inside, I saw that my visit was unjustified because there was Mike, still in bed and next to his head on the pillow was Hokus, sound asleep.

'What about the cage?' I queried.

'I'll need it when I take him home. Till then, it'll stay in the wardrobe where it belongs!'

I have always been against the use of animals in show business, but I must admit, Hokus was one of the few exceptions I'd make. Oddly enough, he ended up bringing much more to our lives than we ever did to his and if you ask me, that's real magic!

33. Stormy Weather

Towards the end of 1984, I was offered the starring role of Tony in a West End production of *West Side Story*. Sadly, when the British Actors' Equity discovered I was not a full-fledged member of their association, they informed the producers that I would not be permitted to perform in the show. I have never been so disappointed in my life, but as I believe that each of us has a pre-traced destiny, I tried not to get too depressed about the situation and waited to see what fate had in store for me. She was not long in revealing her plans, as a few days later I had a phone call from one of the show's producers offering me to head the production shows they had on various cruise ships. I was given the choice of 'Chandris,' a Greek company or 'Paquet,' a French line. I had only recently returned from working on Greek television, so felt drawn to that possibility, but I had finished my studies in French and lived in France for many years, so that option was equally alluring. To help me decide, I asked which of the contracts started first so that I could escape as soon as possible from the predicted harsh European winter.

'*Mermoz* leaves Marseilles on New Year's Day,' came the answer. So that was it. I was starting what was to become a 24 year career in cruising, on Paquet's celebrated flagship.

In the interim, I was called by Paquet's Head of Entertainment to say that he'd cancelled the production show company's contract, but wanted me and Peter to put together a duo so that he could keep us on his roster of artistes. It was too late to do anything else, so we gave in to this latest change of plans and immediately began preparing for our new roles on board.

The company organised our train journey from Normandy to Marseilles via Paris where we were joined by other members of the ship's company. *Mermoz* had been out of service for over a month so that extensive restructuring work could be done at a local shipyard. As we exited the night train, we were quite shocked at the cold nip in the normally balmy air of the French Riviera. Not only was it chilly, but it had snowed the night before and all the tropical orange trees were now covered in a thin layer of ice. The effect of this very rare natural phenomenon was truly magical. The trees sparkled like diamonds in the freezing, but brilliant early morning sunlight. Our taxis pulled up one by one in front of *Mermoz's* berth. She was not yet ready for boarding we were told, and were shown to a large canvas marquee with several folding chairs lining the walls. Had the weather been more clement, this temporary waiting room would have been more than adequate, but with the air temperature hovering around zero degrees Celsius for most of the day, we received little benefit from it.

After several hours of shivering in the bitter cold, we were finally allowed to embark. I hadn't seen what *Mermoz* looked like before her latest refit, but she was very elegant and retained the authentic nautical feel lacking in most of today's cruise ships. There was much speculation as to why we had all been made to wait outside the vessel for such a long time, but as soon as we settled into our cabin, those unsettling rumours lost all of their potency. Disregarding the frigid winds, many passengers lined the ship's railings and threw colourful streamers toward their friends and loved ones braving the winter chill to wave them good-bye.

As soon as *Mermoz* left the relative protection of Marseille's harbour walls, she began to react quite noticeably to the white-capped waves that had churned the Mediterranean Sea into a mass of foam and froth. Those of us new to the sea thought what we were experiencing was about as bad as it could possibly get, short of foundering in the surrounding murky waters. Within an hour, that assumption was proved to be a great underestimation. *Mermoz's* recently reconditioned motors decided to cease functioning, so there was no longer any thrust through the turbulent waters and despite her considerable tonnage, our valiant vessel was tossed about like a leaf on a blustery autumn afternoon. Because the engines had cut out so unexpectedly, the ship's crew had no time to prepare for the violent movement that now shook us with unsettling repetition.

The passengers had all retreated to the safety of their cabins, so mercifully, there were few people around in the public areas when the worst of the storm struck. The grand piano in the newly created Salon Atlantique had been strapped to the bulkhead with thick rope, but at one point *Mermoz's* incline was such that it broke loose and went hurtling across the room. An almighty crash rang out as this beautiful instrument collided with the metal wall to the right of the main entrance. The front leg buckled instantly on impact and the keyboard and hinged lid went flying in every direction. Needless to say, it was a total write-off.

The emergency generators had kept the ship lit and ventilated throughout this ordeal, so it was a few minutes before we realised that the motors had restarted as suddenly as they had stopped. To say that we had smooth sailing all the way to our next port would be a gross exaggeration, but now that the Captain once again had full control, *Mermoz* settled down into a steady, but manageable rocking motion.

Due to the awful weather conditions and time lost during the power-cut, our itinerary had to be altered. After such a bumpy ride, the passengers would have been happy to dock just about anywhere, but Ceuta in Spanish Morocco was where emergency repairs were carried out by the French engineers who had been flown out specially for this vital work to be done before our transatlantic crossing.

Thankfully, the rest of our inaugural cruise and my introduction to the world of cruising passed without incident. I suppose old King Neptune must had decided that if I could serenely deal with such an inauspicious beginning of life on the high seas, then I could be admitted into his elite group of fervent seafarers. It has now been 24 years since that maritime initiation and I happily admit my veins are still full of salt water!

I have been lucky throughout my career at sea because although I get the occasional headache or feel sleepy when the ship rocks too much for too long, I don't suffer from seasickness. My heart goes out to those who are prone to that extreme version of motion sickness, but I couldn't have spent more than two decades travelling around the world on a variety of cruise ships if I felt ill each time the sea got rough.

One very scary moment for me however, happened during a violent storm when I had all the symptoms of seasickness. Had the severe vomiting not started while we were still docked, I may have thought that my constitution had suddenly changed and I was experiencing the same horrible nausea that afflicts many landlubbers when the ship starts to pitch and roll. I was actually suffering from an acute case of food poisoning because I was losing my bodily fluids in every way known to man. I did not want to bother the ship's doctor right away because I knew that I was just one of many cases on board. I hoped that by just resting, I would eventually begin to feel better.

As the hours passed, I was spending more and more time running to the bathroom. I had an unquenchable thirst, but could keep nothing down for more than a few seconds, water included. As I staggered back to my bed I could feel the muscles in my feet start to tighten up. I laid down on the bed and this wave of muscle contractions slowly made its way up my legs. I rang the hospital and told the nurse that I urgently needed to have the doctor visit me. By the time I finished explaining what was wrong with me, I could feel my lips tingling and going numb. It was the most frightening sensation I have ever experienced.

By the time the doctor arrived, my fingers had also gone rigid and were bent back like those of a Balinese dancer. I could no longer speak or move. Thank God the nurse had told the doctor about my unusual symptoms because he was able to put me on a drip laden with calcium. Apparently because of the continual loss of my bodily fluids, I had inadvertently eliminated the calcium in my body and this muscular shutdown was the result. I later learned that had the doctor not intervened as quickly as he did, I may not have survived because the heart is also a muscle and would have eventually reacted like all the other muscles had done. That is as close as I ever want to get to entering the Pearly Gates before my time has really come.

The oldest ship I ever worked on was the *Enrico Costa*, built in 1936. From her very traditional lines, you could see that she was from an era when cruising was in its infancy. Her interior had been refurbished, redesigned and restructured a number of times in her many years of service. Her bridge was all wood-panelled and her helm was the old-fashioned style like you see in the pirate films of Hollywood's heyday. Novice musicians given 'outside cabins' were thrilled when that news reached them via the post, but were totally dismayed when they realised that 'outside' didn't mean the cabin had a porthole, it meant that the cabin door literally opened onto the deck. It wouldn't have been so bad had that part of the deck been covered, but no, the open sky was all that was above their heads when they exited their rooms. There was no problem when the weather was clement, but whenever it rained, the musicians arrived at their cocktail duties soaked to the skin.

For some odd reason, Costa Cruise Line had chosen this ancient vessel for its 'winter sunshine' cruises. We were based in Genoa, sailed down to Barcelona and Majorca before leaving the Mediterranean and heading towards the Atlantic coast of Morocco and the Canary Islands. Many people think that the Mediterranean Sea is constantly bathed in sunshine and her waters are always as tranquil as the proverbial millpond. This may be largely the case in the summer, but winter winds and terrifying tempests hit the 'Med' just like any other part of Europe. If a closed sea like the Mediterranean gets rough in January, imagine what it's like in the Atlantic Ocean! Our cruises lasted 12 days and always followed the same itinerary, so on board we soon learned where to expect the rough patches.

The worst place was at the Straits of Gibraltar. Whenever we left the Mediterranean, a sharp jolt could be felt throughout the ship as though we had run full speed into the Rock itself. This regular welcome to the Atlantic was followed by pitching and rolling all night long until we reached our next port of call.

At the beginning of the season, I vainly tried to schedule a number of shows and cabaret artistes in the main lounge, but no one was able to stand up long enough to perform a full show. After a few futile attempts, I decided just to programme a light classical concert that a talented violinist and I had put together, featuring all the old 'chestnuts' that audiences love to hear time and time again.

The piano was strapped to one of the sturdy pillars on the side of the dance floor so that problem was easily resolved, but I couldn't figure out how to keep the violinist's music stand from constantly falling over. We tried everything but nothing worked, until one night, our social hostess ran onto the floor and caught it just in time. So that it wouldn't move any further during the recital, she draped herself around the stand's vertical pole and sat daintily on two of the three feet. She looked like one of those very romantic sculptured ladies that were used as decorative supports for theatre balconies in the mid-1800s. Her intervention worked so well that I asked her to help out like that on every cruise.

The concert was always a huge success, but it was extremely awkward for our audience to leave the lounge at the end. By that time, the swells outside were so big that even the most experienced sailors found it difficult to move about the vessel unaided. With the help of my entertainment staff we created a human chain, passing the passengers from one person to the next until they reached the safety of the handrails at the back of the room. Oddly enough, no one was ever seasick, they were just bumped about quite a bit.

Music is said to calm the savage beast, but I can assure you, it is absolutely useless for calming the 'white horses' of the Atlantic.

Over the years, passengers have often asked me what was the worst storm I ever experienced. There can only be one answer to that question. It was at the end of a transatlantic crossing on the very exclusive *Silver Wind*. We had enjoyed a relatively tranquil voyage from our berth on the Thames in the heart of London to the eastern coast of the United States, so everyone was surprised when the captain requested that all the passengers attend a special meeting in the theatre concerning the weather forecast for the next 24 hours. He had brought some very detailed nautical charts with him and as he proceeded to point out the assumed trajectory of Hurricane Marilyn, an eerie stillness filled the auditorium.

'About 99 percent of hurricanes follow the coast in a northerly direction, then at some point, head out to sea where they lose their potency and die out,' said the captain reassuringly. 'The United States Coast Guard has told us that if we sail southwards until we reach the American coastline, then stay at a safe distance from the edge of the storm and follow her northward, we should experience nothing more that the slight swell we're feeling at the present. Thank you all for attending this brief meeting. Of course, I'll keep you informed should any new developments arise,' he added as he began carefully folding up his charts.

The room was instantly filled with the relaxed chatter of people who had just been given an unexpected reprieve by a lenient judge. For the rest of the day, life on board continued in a jovial and happy atmosphere despite the constant rocking of our relatively small ship. After the last couples had cleared the dance floor and the barmen had finished tidying up for the night, *Silver Wind* fell silent as she journeyed onward towards New York City.

I awoke early the following morning to try to catch up on my paperwork so that I could have some free time in New York to visit with my family. Whenever we were at sea it was the captain's habit to make a 9.00am announcement from the bridge to talk about the weather, give the ship's bearings and inform us of any interesting things we might be passing during the day, so no one was startled to hear the familiar 'bing bong' ring over the loudspeakers at precisely nine o'clock.

'Good morning, Ladies and Gentlemen. This is the captain. I trust everyone slept well and is now enjoying a hearty breakfast in the dining room. As promised during yesterday's impromptu meeting, it is my intention to keep you all informed concerning the prevailing inclement weather conditions here in the North Atlantic; therefore, I'd like to invite all guests to meet me in the main theatre at ten o'clock this morning for an update on the situation. Thank you for your attention, and enjoy your breakfast,' the captain concluded in his usual ebullient voice.

I arrived early to check that our stage hands had properly prepared everything for the captain's speech and was taken aback to see that he was already there, thumbing through a stack of papers. The concerned look on his face was in direct contradiction to the cheery voice heard on the tannoy only an hour earlier. I made my way across the quickly filling auditorium to see if I could be of any assistance. Before I said anything, he suddenly turned around.

'Oh good, Gary. It's you,' he said. 'I'll need your help over the next 24 hours.'

'Of course, Captain. You can count on me to do whatever you need,' I answered, immediately perceiving the unspoken danger he was alluding to.

'Wouldn't you know it? Almost all of these hurricanes peter out as they head north but this son of a b**** has to break all the rules,' he mumbled to himself as he continued to fiddle about with his paperwork.

'Is there anything I can do for you now, sir?' I inquired. He looked at his watch, then turned to me.

'Yes,' he said. 'Just announce me to the passengers. We'd better get this show on the road so I can get back to the bridge.'

The warm applause that greeted the captain as he took the stage soon turned into a stunned silence. You could see it on everyone's face: real, raw fear as he explained that Hurricane Marilyn had unexpectedly reversed direction, picking up considerable speed and wind force as she headed southwards.

'Unfortunately, there is no port large enough for us to take shelter in before the hurricane reaches us, so I'm afraid we're just going to have to sail right into her,' the captain stated in a very matter-of-fact manner. 'By lunchtime today, I expect the seas to be quite rough, so for those of you who are not good sailors or are not stable on your feet, I suggest you stay in your cabins and take a seasickness tablet as soon as this meeting is finished. I will continue to keep you all informed about the hurricane's progress throughout the day and the Cruise Director here will explain what entertainment will be available to you today. Thank you for your attention and for attending this meeting,' he said with a gravity that showed as much on his face as it was evident in his voice.

As soon as I reached the centre of the stage, everyone stopped talking and looked up at me with eyes full of hope. 'Ladies and Gentlemen, obviously all outside activities will have to be cancelled due to the rising winds, but as long as it is safe to do so, we plan to continue with our full entertainment schedule as printed in your daily programme. In consultation with the bridge, I'll keep you informed though our public address system should any event have to be called off or should there be any change in our mealtimes. Please remember that should anyone require any assistance, medical or otherwise, our reception is manned 24 hours a day. Thank you for your attention, Ladies and Gentlemen, and let's all try to enjoy today as much as is possible' I said, trying to sound cheerfully optimistic.

By lunchtime, it was clear that only those who were natural cruisers were still out and about. The rest had taken the captain's advice and gone to bed. By 2.00pm, we were experiencing waves of up to 60 feet in height. The whole ship was carried to dizzying heights and then dropped down into the bottom of a trough of water. At these points, the water on either side of the vessel was higher than she was, but on we sailed.

This crossing was one of Silversea's well-loved celebrity cruises where stars of yesteryear regaled the ship's passengers with behind-the-scenes stories of their fabulous careers and gave intimate details of their often scandalous personal lives. On the day of the storm, I was to interview Hope Lange, the lovely leading lady of the 1950s and 60s. Everyone remembered her for her portrayals in iconic films like *Bus Stop* with Marilyn Monroe or her popular television work in the film spin-off *The Ghost and Mrs. Muir*. She must have been in her sixties at the time, but had kept her figure and allure. She found the whole hurricane business quite entertaining and insisted that we do her interview as planned.

To my astonishment, the theatre was almost full, so rather unsteadily, Hope and I made our way arm-in-arm towards the two plush chairs that had been placed centre-stage for us. Once we were comfortably seated, I began the interview by thanking both my guest star and the audience for showing up. I informed everyone that this informal chat would be tape-recorded and shown at a later date on the ship's closed-circuit television channel should anyone have to leave before the end.

I thought I saw Hope's armchair move slightly each time I looked down at my notepad to ask the next question, but each time I looked up, she was completely immobile, so I assumed it must be some sort of sense distortion due to the excess motion of the ship. This little 'optical illusion' continued until totally by surprise, she and the chair went gliding past me just as she began to speak.

'Whee!' she cried as she reached the wings of the stage. Before she could grab hold of anything, the ship rolled the other way, and she was off again, sailing by me at such a speed that I had no time to react. My own chair never budged an inch, but then my height and weight played in my favour that day. Hope could not have been taller than five foot three or four at the most and was very slender. She looked like a young bird as she 'flew' gracefully back and forth across the wooden stage. The audience loved this little bit of unplanned visual comedy and were laughing louder and louder with each 'flight'. On her fourth 'crossing' I managed to take hold of the back of her chair, but the force of it literally pulled me out of my own. As we both went sailing into the curtains at the side of the stage I wrapped one arm around them and the other around Hope. We then crawled on ' all fours' until we reached the edge of the stage. By now, the passengers were screaming with laughter and Hope and I were giggling like two school children as well, fully realising how ridiculous we must have looked.

Once we were finally safely perched on the rim of the stage, we sat there huddled together, swaying to and fro in time to the waves that continued to batter our ship. Hope was a wonderful subject to interview and had many funny stories to tell. There were just as many poignant moments when she spoke of the heartaches that had also left their mark on her life. Just as everyone was awkwardly trying to leave the theatre at the end of the interview, we all froze as we heard the bells of the public address system ring.

'Ladies and Gentlemen, this is the captain. I'm happy to inform you that the worst of the storm is now behind us. We will however, continue to experience very strong winds and high waves for the rest of the evening, but thankfully, with decreasing intensity as the night progresses. We'll be arriving at New York City one full day late, but I know you are as grateful as I am that *Silver Wind* has shown her true colours throughout this ordeal with minimal damage. A service of thanksgiving will be held tomorrow morning in the theatre for all who wish to attend. Thank you for your patience and understanding. I wish you all a most peaceful evening.'

The following morning, there was not a free seat to be had, as guests and crew members crowded around the doorways to the theatre to take part in the brief service led by the captain. As we all sang the traditional sailors' hymn *Eternal Father Strong to Save* and reached the words 'Oh hear us when we cry to Thee for those in peril on the sea,' I saw many of the officers lower their heads and discreetly wipe the tears from their eyes, the captain included.

When we passed the majestic Statue of Liberty later that day at the entrance to New York harbour, I read over the ship's loud speakers the stirring words of Emma Lazarus' poem that this symbol of freedom is known for around the world:

Give me your tired, your poor, your huddled masses yearning to breathe free; the wretched refuse of your teeming shores, send these: the homeless, tempest tossed to me. I lift my lamp beside the golden door.

On deck and around the ship, the end of the poem was met with reverential silence and many an emotional lump in the throat. Then, all of a sudden, spontaneous, loud cheering was heard throughout the vessel.

Everyone on board had just come through one of the most terrifying experiences at sea, yet this brief brush with disaster and possible death seemed insignificant compared to the intense hardship and inspirational bravery of those who had left their homelands over a century ago to begin life anew in a foreign country. The legacy of those courageous people never fails to touch the hearts of those who sail by 'Lady Liberty,' and the passengers of *Silver Wind* were no exception. Moments like that have a way of putting one's own trials and tribulations into perspective, and a sense of gratitude and humility are the gifts bestowed upon those who are sensitive enough to receive them.

34. Simple Pleasures

Many things that are taken for granted on today's luxury liners were either unheard of or reserved only for the first class guests on board in days gone by. Communal bathrooms were the norm for the crew and even for second or tourist class passengers in the not-so-distant past. Proper theatres were few and far between, so most shows and activities were held in the ship's main ballroom. In addition to their evening performances, cabaret artistes often ran everything from the shuffleboard tournaments to the afternoon bingo sessions. In earlier times still, the purser's department would be responsible for those activities, as well as much of the evening entertainment. Crepe paper and balloons were the cruise staff's best friends as these basic materials could not only be used to create exotic costumes for the passengers, they could also transform the ship's lounges to reflect a myriad of popular themes. Halloween parties, masquerade balls and Santa's Christmas grotto are just a few of the events that inspired the teams to display their creative talents to the full.

Somehow, the passengers were more than happy with this simple, homespun entertainment and many of today's older cruisers still mourn the passing of those gentler times.

One of the most requested theme evenings was and still is, a 1950s and 60s Rock and Roll Night. There is something about the great music and flamboyant fashions of those iconic decades that rekindles nostalgia in the hearts of those who lived through them and incites the younger generations to want to experience them, if only for an hour or so.

On one of Costa Cruise Lines' smaller vessels, the *Costa Allegra*, a 50s and 60s Night was an integral part of our entertainment package throughout the summer of 1993. We had been given free rein by Costa's entertainment department to develop this event however we wanted, so after a series of brainstorming meetings, our team came up with what turned out to be one of the most successful celebrations of that wonderful era on the high seas.

Although a portion of the overall success depended somewhat on the choice of our participants, the formula was almost foolproof and we could always count on at least one or two natural comedians in the audience. We were fortunate enough to have Julie Grant on board with us that summer as one of the star production singers. Julie was a great team player, so it didn't take long to convince her to kick off the proceedings by singing *Up on the Roof*, one of her big hits of the 1960s. After that auspicious opening, our contestants were given points for a number of 50s and 60s-related challenges. They had to keep a hula-hoop spinning for one full minute. The ladies tended to be good at this, whereas the men were generally comically uncoordinated. There was a yo-yo contest, a jitterbug/jive dance-off and a musical quiz entitled *Name that Hit Song*. How points should be awarded for some parts of the evening was quite obvious, but other sections like the dance contest needed the audience's input to see how each couple fared. In addition to performing as half of the song and dance duo *Glading and Allan*, Peter also worked as my Assistant Cruise Director. As such he was a bit of a mad genius and could make the most wonderful things out of scrap pieces of cardboard, cellotape and coloured pens. We decided that we needed an 'applausometre' to measure the level of the appreciation shown by the audience for each of our participating couples.

We had no real budget for this kind of thing, so Peter just made a quick tour of the ship, collecting various bits and pieces along the way. He returned to the office with what looked like a pile of rubbish, but within an hour, the cardboard box, the empty mineral water bottles, the aluminium foil, the string and the light bulbs had been ingeniously put together to resemble the laboratory equipment Vincent Price used in many of his horror films. The idea was that Peter arrived on stage with this wonderful piece of pseudo-1950's technology and I asked the passengers to help me test it to make sure it was working. At the beginning I asked the guests to applaud softly and then increase the volume. In theory, the arrow on the dial of the machine was meant to move from zero to 100, according to the intensity of the applause, but to have a little silly fun, at first, the machine did not work. I looked at Peter standing there scratching his head in befuddlement. After a second or two, he would suddenly brighten up as if he had just had an inspiring thought and pick up the end of a long electric cord showing it to the audience. A good laugh here was a real certainty. As soon as the machine was 'plugged in', we proceeded with the test and with the help of Peter's hand inside the back of the box, the arrow magically moved up and down to reflect the volume of the clapping made by the passengers.

In order to avoid choosing a winning couple and thus, disappoint all the other contestants that had entertained the guests all evening long, Peter always made sure that the applausometre 'exploded' before we reached the final couple. This made it impossible to fairly judge those participants, so we could legitimately reward everyone with a nice ship's prize.

At the beginning of the season, the explosion was made by inserting a microphone in the back of the box so that Peter's bursting of a balloon next to it was heard all over the room. I thought it was rather effective, but Peter was not satisfied, so on each cruise there was an enhanced version of the explosion to look forward to. Most of the variations were on the amount and origins of the smoke that accompanied the 'boom' made by the popping balloon. The whole inside of the cardboard box was covered with a sheet of aluminium foil, making it fireproof, so I just let Peter experiment with his smoke-making trials.

One of the most effective devices was a small cube sold in magic shops that produced dark smoke when lit. The only drawback with it was that the smoke tended to pour out of the back of the box and gather along the floor behind the table. It didn't create the visual impact Peter was looking for. Another impressive attempt was when Peter brought back some incense from a Bulgarian orthodox church. A round charcoal pellet had to be lit and that in turn ignited the heavily perfumed incense. I thought it looked brilliant, but our resident mad scientist was still not convinced he had reached the zenith of his creative powers.

On the final 1950s and 60s night of the season, Peter pulled out all the stops. The original box had been enlarged and upgraded so many times that it was no longer recognisable from its humble beginnings. We had a particularly enthusiastic crowd in for our game show and the contestants were some of the best we had seen. The beginning of the applausometre gag remained unchanged, with the electric cord being plugged in and the trial runs 'proving' that the monstrosity actually worked. Then came the judging of the first few couples. Everything was going like clockwork; however, the tension in the team mounted as we awaited the grand finale, knowing Peter had been feverishly working to complete it. Finally the moment of the explosion arrived. The amplified 'pop' was particularly loud, with many ladies in the audience screaming and jumping out of their seats such was its impact. True to form, Peter smiled broadly as smoke came billowing out of the top of the applausometre. No one was ready for what happened next. Suddenly, little pieces of newspaper started to float out of the back of the box and rise into the air. Normally that would not have been a problem, but they were still on fire! Carlotta, our social hostess was standing next to the box. She was supposed to be our glamorous assistant in the nostalgic games played by our contestants, but her reaction to this turn of events was anything but glamorous. As soon as she realised that the paper was still aflame and after a short flight upwards was falling onto the stage, she began performing a sort of demonic tarantella, desperately trying to stamp out the mini-barbecues that were now scattered about the floor. It was obvious to me that the tiny bits of paper would burn out before they became a dangerous threat to the ship, but to our Neapolitan dancing dervish, she was single-handedly saving the lives of everyone on board, her own included. Even the audience could see that there was no cause for concern and before long everyone was convulsed with laughter at the sight of this normally placid lady cavorting about the stage as if she were possessed by some evil spirit from the netherworld.

The fun would have ended sooner had she not been wearing rubber-soled shoes. To the great delight of her mesmerised spectators, a big wad of burning paper stuck to the bottom of her shoe and actually set it alight. Her rhythmic tarantella now became a frantic fandango as she hopped and skipped around the stage like a demented schoolgirl on LSD. You may wonder why Peter or I didn't come to the rescue of this Italian 'Joan of Arc' who was burning before our very eyes. In all honesty, the two of us were literally paralysed with laughter. The scene was so comical that neither of us could do anything more than wipe the tears from our eyes and hold our shaking sides. This unforeseen ending to a most enjoyable game show merited the full standing ovation that our social hostess received when the last lick of fire was extinguished and her smouldering shoe was doused in a bucket of water provided by one of the stagehands. Our passengers spoke of little else for the rest of the cruise.

So many things happen every day on a cruise ship that, memorable as it was, that fun-filled night was soon forgotten, until one of the British passengers sent Carlotta a gift. We all crowded around her as she opened the box in our entertainment office. As she pulled back the tissue paper surrounding the contents we all burst out laughing. There inside the box was a new pair of shoes. Inside one of them was a box of matches and inside the other was a rolled up ball of newspaper. There was a little note saying 'You light my sole on fire.'

Ah, for the good old days!

35. Stars That Have Lit Up My Sky

For most of my career at sea I have worked for international cruise lines where it is not uncommon to work in five or six languages. I have always enjoyed the exciting multi-cultural aspects of that type of cruising because one minute I would be in an all-French environment and the next, downing a tankard of lager with the German-speakers on board. Entertaining such a diverse group of passengers was not without its problems but success (when it came) tasted very sweet because the challenges were so great and so many. The main thing I missed was being able to use humour when presenting the shows or games, simply because it is not possible to translate a joke quickly and effectively in five languages without boring the socks off everyone who doesn't work for the United Nations.

When I started to work for P&O Cruises almost three years ago, it felt quite strange at first to only use one language to communicate with the passengers, but any initial awkwardness soon turned into pure joy. It was absolutely wonderful to entertain audiences that not only shared a common language but had a common culture and history as well. These assets allowed me to develop a complete entertainment programme for our guests that I have thoroughly enjoyed being involved with ever since.

One of the greatest benefits of using just one language has allowed me to interview the many high profile celebrities of show business, politics and sport that the company sent on board as after-dinner speakers. All were household names, so the theatre was always full when these personalities spoke or I was called upon to interview them. Regardless of your politics, who would not be excited about the opportunity to speak to former Deputy Prime Minister Lord Geoffrey Howe and to hear first hand all about the infamous speech he made to Parliament that ultimately led to Margaret Thatcher's downfall? Lord Steele was another gifted speaker who packed the theatre to the rafters. The audience responded warmly to him and were appreciative of his candour as he answered their questions at the end of his talk. After the event was over and most passengers had left the room, I was stopped by an elderly lady who seemed to be waiting for me. As I approached her she said sourly, 'I sat through his entire speech and not once did he mention any of his films or West End musicals. I suppose he doesn't want his constituents to know about his show business background.'

'You must be thinking of Tommy Steele,' I countered. 'That was David Steele who just spoke.'

'Well, you'd at least think he would make some reference to his brother,' she replied. 'There's no shame in singing and dancing, you know.'

For someone who has been in show business as long as I have, presenting West End star Marti Webb to our passengers one New Year's Eve was truly unforgettable. After singing her way through every one of her hits from *Don't Cry for Me Argentina* to *Take that Look off your Face* to *Tell Me on a Sunday*, the audience rose to their feet and erupted in some of the loudest cheering I have ever heard. For our interview the following afternoon, people were sitting in the aisles, cramming the entrances and even crouching down on the floor in front of the stage. Marti is so 'under-whelmed' by her own career that she talks about Andrew Lloyd Webber, Tim Rice and Cameron Macintosh like you or I would talk about our favourite auntie or friend. The passengers hung on to every word of every anecdote she told. This kind of event would not have been possible without the common language and shared cultural heritage I spoke of earlier.

Another singing phenomenon that greatly impressed me during her performances and throughout our interview was the Welsh star Iris Williams. She was deservedly awarded an OBE in 2004 for her extensive charity work and for her exemplary contribution to show business, yet is one of the most warm and unaffected people I have ever met. In life, fate often has an odd way of working things out, respecting none of the rules of conventional behaviour.

Back in the summer of 1980, I was the lead singer in a travelling show organised by the famous Paris Lido, home to the celebrated Bluebell Girls. We were touring the British Isles and the Republic of Ireland to publicise Miss Bluebell's autobiography and her up-coming appearance as Eamonn Andrews' special guest on *This is Your Life*. One afternoon as I was busily composing a new song in one of the theatres we were performing in, Jean Régile the show's French magician walked in unnoticed by me. When I finished playing the new piece through, he began to applaud. He asked me what the name of the song was as he had never heard it before. I explained that it was something I was working on for French television. 'You mean you're a composer?' he queried.

'Yes, I am. Why do you ask?' I replied.

'Well, Iris Williams a dear friend of mine was just awarded a gold record for the song *He Was Beautiful* and she's looking for a follow-up hit. I think you may be just the person she needs. Would you like to meet her?' he asked.

'I'd be delighted,' I answered.

A few phone calls later and a date was set for the following Sunday in Torquay where Iris Williams was playing to packed houses at the Barbican Theatre. Clive, her husband/manager had prepared a fabulous meal and the table conversation was jovial and relaxed. When we finished, Iris suggested I play my songs for her.

Despite her obvious concentration I could tell by the twinkle in her eye and the smile on her face that she liked what she heard.

'Gary, your songs are absolutely beautiful. They are just what I'm looking for. If you're not in a hurry, I think it would be a good idea to call my record producer right away to set up an appointment for him to hear them as soon as possible,' Iris said.

'That's great. There's no hurry whatsoever. I can always catch a later train if I miss the one I was planning to take,' I replied.

I felt like I was in some kind of dream. This highly successful singer not only liked my songs, she was planning to record them! I could hardly believe it.

'Hello Wally, this is Iris,' she said in that warm, deep voice that has made her famous. 'I'm sorry to bother you on a Sunday, Wally, but I've just met a very talented young composer who has played the most marvellous songs for me and I'd like you to hear him as soon as possible.'

From that point onwards, Iris couldn't manage a full sentence. I could tell from her one word answers that Wally was making it clear that *he* would be the one to make the new discoveries and that *he* would decide what she would sing and when, because *he* had made her the star she had become.

Before either of us realised what was happening, Clive grabbed the phone out her hand and told the producer that he was fed up with his interference in his wife's career and that Wally would see me or else! That seemed to work, at least temporarily, because when Clive hung up, he told me that I was to be at the EMI offices the following Sunday to meet Mr Ridley. Looking at his watch he said we'd better get a move on, otherwise I would miss my train. As I was saying good-bye to Iris, she said, 'I love your ballads very much, but would you do me a favour?'

'Of course,' I replied instinctively.

'Waltzes have always brought me good luck. Would you write a waltz… just for me?'

'Consider it done,' I said, jumping into the car.

That was the last I saw of Iris Williams for 28 years. Yes, I did go to EMI as planned, but when Wally Ridley greeted me at the door of his office with 'You've wasted your time, young man,' I knew that he was right.

Two summers ago, I was Cruise Director on P&O Cruises' elegant ship *Oriana*. A few weeks before each cruise our Southampton office sends us a list of all the entertainers that are embarking on any given cruise. Sometime in July I received just such a list and saw the name Iris Williams at the very top, meaning she was to be our VIP guest star for that cruise. It's strange how a whole forgotten period of time can be instantly recalled when something like that triggers off memories. I could hardly wait to meet her and see if she remembered our brief encounter during the summer of 1980.

Certain things in life are not fair, and the fact that Iris looked exactly as she had 28 years earlier made me realise just how much I had changed over the years. Gone was the hope that she would recognise me, or so I thought. I invited her for a coffee to discuss the programming of her shows and our interview. You don't have to be exceptionally sensitive to know when someone is really studying you, trying to figure out where they have seen you before. After a few minutes of such scrutiny Iris sweetly asked, 'Haven't we met before?'

'Yes,' I answered coyly, '28 years ago.'

'What?' she shrieked, her reaction surprising both of us. I related the events of the summer of 1980 and she just sat there, astounded at all the detail I recalled. I described the house she had rented, where the dining room was, where the piano was placed and so on.

She laughed when I reminded her that she had requested I write a waltz for her because they always brought her good luck.

'Well, did you write me a waltz?' she asked.

'Of course I did,' I confirmed. 'Would you like to hear it?'

'I think 28 years is long enough to wait, don't you?' she said with a teasing look in her eye.

When I finished playing the song she had inspired, she said softly, 'Wally would have loved that one, you know. He would have recorded it in a heartbeat.' Then she snapped out of her reverie and said 'What are the lyrics like?'

My heart stood still. Yes, I had written the melody I had just played, but when our recording plans fell through, I never bothered to write any words to the haunting tune. For years I used it as an encore piece at the end of my classical piano recitals and introduced it as *Nostalgie*. I knew I had to bargain for some time, so I nonchalantly replied, 'Oh, I'll have to look in my computer archives. I must have them somewhere.'

That night I couldn't get to sleep. In my head I kept hearing Iris asking me for the lyrics, so I just got up and began to write. The next morning after several cups of very strong coffee, I rang Iris' cabin and invited her to hear the completed song. She fell in love with it and I am thrilled to say, so has every audience that has heard her incomparable singing of it since.

It wasn't long before I confessed to Iris about the 28-year gap between the composing of the music and the writing of the lyrics. Her response was typical of the delightful lady she is, 'Wow, that is quite a long time to be in labour, but what a beautiful baby you've given me! Thank you, Gary.'

I am delighted to report that Iris recorded my song *Once in Each Life* in early 2011. It is featured on her latest album *Catch My Dreams*.

Here's hoping the waltz she requested all those years ago brings her all the luck in the world.

Other celebrity guests it has been my pleasure to meet and an honour to interview are television icon Esther Rantzen, news broadcaster Peter Snow and his talented son Dan, soap actress and star of *Loose Women* Sherrie Hewson and actor/writer/producer George Layton. Each one of these warm and exceptionally gifted people gave our audiences an unforgettable hour or so in their presence. It was easy to understand why each guest had become successful and remained popular with the British public for so long. I was grateful for the many lunches, dinners, coffees and cocktails we had together as we got to know each other better and prepared our upcoming informal interviews.

It is hard to select just one or two people from such an illustrious list of well-known personalities, but I would be remiss if I did not write about legendary footballer Jack Charlton. Every schoolboy of my generation as well as his dad, uncles and friends practically worshipped the ground Jackie and Bobby Charlton walked on, so it is easy to imagine how nervous I felt when I recently met Jack Charlton, OBE. Jack's friendly personality and down-to-earth Geordie approach to life made my fears melt away in the warmth of his presence. A minute or two before Jack's first talk, he asked me if it was all right if he swore. Stupidly I said, 'What, now?'

'No, during my talk.' he answered laughing. Before I could reply he continued, 'Last summer, the Cruise Director said, "Absolutely no swearing, Jack...company policy, you know." What do *you* think, Gary?' he challenged.

I knew he was testing me here, but I also knew my passengers. People who had come to hear about the life and times of Jack Charlton were football fans, so I felt sure they would not be offended if they heard a few mild oaths from one of their heroes.

'Jack,' I said. 'As far as I'm concerned, you could get away with murder and this crowd would applaud you for it. Just go out there and be yourself. They'll love you whatever you say or do.'

'That's grand. I won't let you down,' he assured me.

I had to literally step over his fans to reach the stage, such was the density of the crowd that turned out to hear him speak. After a brief, but stirring introduction, I turned the microphone over to Jack. When the spontaneous applause finally died down he announced, 'I'm gonna swear in this talk, so if you're offended by that sort of thing, you'd better leave now. I'm not going to swear just for the sake of it, the swearing will be an important part of the stories I'm going to tell you, and they just wouldn't make sense if I replaced the swear words with other ones. I'll give you an example.' This he did, and when he finished his short tale by saying that someone thought he was a real 'twat,' the entire audience roared with laughter. He and I both knew he had them in his pocket. A cheeky wink in my direction confirmed it and my 'thumbs up' encouraged him to give one of the best talks I have ever heard. After one hour and fifteen minutes, he finally wrapped up what was an unmitigated triumph. There was no need for me to remind those in attendance that Jack would be giving two further talks and an interview with me before the end of the cruise, because each of those events was as popular and well-attended as the first. This was not only a fitting tribute to his incredible career, but also to his natural talent as a public speaker.

I'd like to finish this chapter on some of the wonderful VIPs I have met thanks to P&O Cruises, by relating a very touching incident which involved Jack Charlton.

On the same cruise where Jack was our celebrity guest speaker we had a young Liverpudlian singer booked to make his debut with our company. He was as mad on football as he was keen to make a positive impression on our passengers. That Jack Charlton was not only on board to give three talks, but that his childhood hero would hear him sing made the lad from Liverpool as happy as anyone could possibly be. Then, three days before his first show, our young crooner collapsed while crossing one of the public lounges. He was taken directly to the ship's hospital and I was immediately apprised of the situation. I went straight down to the infirmary and found him looking very pale and vulnerable. He tried to put on a brave face, but the senior doctor explained to me that the young man had suffered a collapsed lung and would not be able to perform for the rest of the cruise. I was assured that everything would be done to keep him on board, but if the lung did not re-inflate within a few days, he would have to be transferred to a hospital on land for possible surgery. Unfortunately, the singer's attack happened the day before Jack Charlton's first talk, so not only would he not be able to sing for his hero, he would never even have the chance to meet him or hear him talk about his legendary career.

I waited until Jack had finished his first wildly successful presentation in the theatre to broach the subject. After he had shaken the last hand and signed the final autograph of the day I took Jack and his charming wife for a drink to wind down a bit. Once the euphoria of his resounding performance had begun to wear off, I explained to the Charltons what had happened to our young entertainer and how desolated he was not to have attended Jack's talk. Before I could go any further, Jack said, 'Why don't I just go down to the hospital and do it all again for the lad? Would that be all right?'

For once, I was completely speechless. After a moment or two I managed to say that I would have a quiet word with the doctor and see if and when this might be possible.

Later that evening I rang Jack and told him that the doctor felt a 20-minute visit was about all the poor lad could handle as he was not responding to the treatment as well as had been hoped for. I met Jack and his wife for coffee the following morning and then Jack and I went down to the hospital. Although I had been making several short visits a day to see our patient, I never mentioned Jack's offer, so when he and I strolled into the sick bay, I thought our young entertainer was going to have a stroke. Jack walked straight over to the bed, stretched out his hand.

'Hello, son,' he said. 'I'm Jack Charlton. I heard you've been poorly and thought I just drop by to see how you're doing.'

The young singer's face went bright red and his eyes welled-up as he tried to say 'thank you for coming.' Jack is such a great man that within seconds he had the lad totally relaxed, chatting away about football.

Then the head nurse arrived with a clipboard in her hand.

'I hope you've all enjoyed your visit because I'm afraid we must call it a day now,' she said as she motioned towards the open door. 'Our young man here needs to have some rest before his exams this afternoon. I'm sure you understand, gentlemen,'

'Of course,' we said in unison.

'Bye, bye, son. You look after yourself. I'll be back as soon as you're feeling a little better,' called out Jack as the nurse closed the door behind us.

Sadly, Jack never had the chance to see him again because early the following morning the lad had to be transported to a specialised clinic ashore for immediate surgery. A week later, we received an e-mail from our young singer, saying that he was on the mend and wished to thank everyone who had been so kind to him whilst he was on board. He ended with, 'Please thank Jack for me, Gary. Tell him he'll never know how much his visit meant to me.'

When I told Jack what his young friend had written, I could see clearly that he was both relieved at the good news and moved by the sentiments the lad had expressed. He lowered his head and muttered humbly, 'It was nothing.'

How wrong he was!

36. From Pirates to Pets

When I first started out in cruising, there were less rules and regulations to follow so it was not unusual for passengers or even some of the senior crew members, the captain included, to have a small pet on board. All that was required was a proper health certificate for the animal to show to the local port authorities upon request. This flexibility allowed me to rescue half a dozen cats and to look after tired, ill or wounded sea birds with total impunity. In recent years, a plethora of new laws and their stringent application has made all of that impossible. It has not, however, dampened my ardour for animal welfare and I continue to take food ashore to feed the stray cats and dogs that still inhabit the quaysides of the poorer countries of the world.

During the first three months of 2009, I was Cruise Director on P&O Cruises' luxury liner *Arcadia* as she made her inaugural Grand Voyage out to the Far East and back to her home port of Southampton. This meant transiting the Suez Canal and sailing through the Gulf of Aden at both the beginning and the end of the 101-day trip. Piracy in that part of the world has increased dramatically over the past few years and just two weeks before we reached the area on our homeward journey, heavily armed Somali pirates attacked another cruise ship. Luckily for us, we were escorted by a ship of the Royal Navy on the way out, and had helicopter coverage on the way back. Thank God for the red ensign we flew and the brave people who man Her Majesty's fleet.

I have been to Egypt numerous times and have visited all of the wonderful archaeological splendours of her glorious past, so these days prefer to allow my younger staff members to accompany the passenger excursions so they too can experience these ancient treasures first hand. For me, Egypt now means the chance to do some good for all of the feral animals that populate the port areas of that fascinating country. *Arcadia* arrived early one morning in Safaga so that passengers and crew could have a full day to visit the famous monuments of Luxor and the Valley of the Kings.

This gave me the opportunity of taking some food out to the 30 or 40 dogs that were roaming around the dock in search of something to eat. I whistled loudly to call them to a remote corner of the parking lot and they all followed me with tails wagging in anticipation. Although painfully thin, I could see that they were all basically healthy animals who shared a family resemblance. There was definitely a pecking order and they all seemed to know their place. A second feeding session took place again late afternoon when the sun wasn't so intense and the attendance was more or less the same as at breakfast time. By late evening I could see all the dogs queued up once more, waiting for their supper to be brought out to them.

Our executive chef was an Irishman with a heart as big as the galley he commanded. He knew all about my animal welfare work so told me where I could pick up bags of uneaten sausage rolls and other scraps. I happened to bump into him again as we were heading for our respective cabins to change for the evening. 'You know we can only keep food on the buffet upstairs for a limited time. If you play your cards right, your four-legged friends might just get some spare ribs for dinner tonight,' he said with a grin.

I did play my cards right and showed up with several empty bags to fill. My Egyptian canine pals could smell the meat as soon as I reached the top of the gangway. Their barking was enough to bring the mummies back to life. Once the last dog had received his portion of the spare ribs I turned around to head back to the ship. Looking up at our beautifully lit-up ship I saw the promenade deck was lined with passengers who were waving and applauding as I hurried back inside. Many of them were dropping bits of food over the side for the dogs who had already finished their meat rations. It was heart-warming to see such good will towards these poor creatures.

Port Said was our next stop and instead of dogs, I found only cats along the quay. My feeding routine was much the same as it had been two days before except I had to be careful about which meat had bones still attached. As dusk was falling and I had welcomed the last passenger back on board a little kitten ran up to me and began to rub itself against my leg. He looked exactly like a cat I had rescued in that same port 23 years earlier. How my heart broke as I made my way up the gangway, leaving him staring after me as I entered the ship. Then I had a brilliant idea to give him a proper send-off. I took the lift straight up to the buffet and filled a plate with sliced beef and turkey. I wrapped the meat up in paper napkins and ran out onto the open deck. By this point we were already several feet away from the dock so I rolled a few pieces of meat into a ball and threw it as hard as I could. As it hit the concrete quayside, it exploded, sending bits of meat flying in various directions. The poor kitten didn't know which way to run first. By the time I had launched the last nutritious package, my little feline friend had settled down and was busily chewing away at this tangible sign of affection that had fallen from the skies.

As I mentioned earlier, the animals I saw this year in Egypt all looked emaciated, but there were no signs of illness. Their teeth and gums looked healthy as did their coats. This is a huge difference from what I used to see even five or six years ago. It seems that whenever ships dock in these harbours other kind people are doing their bit to feed these hungry creatures. Days like those I have described when you are confronted by so much need can be overwhelming and depressing. Or they can be opportunities to do a little good by sharing what we have. We all have the choice…

37. And Finally…..

As I wrote in the introduction to this book, cruising has changed beyond all recognition in the 26 years of my involvement in this fascinating and highly competitive industry. Large, multi-branded companies have swallowed up the small family-run businesses of the past. In the long run, this pheonemeon has instigated opening up the once prestigious world of cruising to younger generations and less affluent travelers across the globe. Ports that used to berth one or two cruise ships a month are now invaded by dozens of floating behemoths every week.

Although the future of cruising looks positive and encouraging, I have lived through the frightening times following 9/11, the Chernobyl disaster and the outbreak of a variety of viruses that have threatened to bring this tourism giant to its knees. Most shipyards have a full order book for the next few years and the majority of cruise lines are carrying through aggressive expansion policies. That said, one major international incident could easily bring this fragile house of cards crashing down. If this sounds like the plot of a modern novel, perhaps it is, but whatever the future holds for cruising and travel in general, the thing that makes it all work is us; the people who are eager for discovery and adventure. So wherever your wanderlust takes you, may your seas be calm, your journeys enlightening and your thirst for knowledge unquenchable.

About the Author

Gary Glading trained in classical music in America and at the Le Conservatoire de Musique in Lausanne. After receiving his Master's degree, he was 'discovered' by Marlene Dietrich and hired by the famous Paris Lido to open their new show in Las Vegas where he worked alongside many of America's legendary performers. He returned to Paris to star in the original Lido show on the Champs Elysees and to take part in television shows with such greats as Ginger Rogers, Shirley MacLaine, Tom Jones and Sacha Distel.

Gary's life at sea began on New Year's Day in 1985, when along with his professional partner British dancer Peter Allan, he accepted an offer to perform a two man song and dance show on a French cruise ship. Since then he has been an entertainer, cruise director, production show writer/producer as well as Director of Entertainment for a wide variety of cruise companies. Gary has also appeared regularly on television and written plays and articles for travel and animal welfare publications. His work on cruise ships has given him the opportunity to interview and get to know many well known stars from the worlds of showbusiness and sport.

Fluent in eight languages, Gary is now a Cruise Director/Entertainer for NCL after three years with P&O Cruises. He lives in Italy where he runs a sanctuary for abandoned and abused animals.